Mar Alexander Del

A History Of Monetary Crimes

Mar Alexander Del

A History Of Monetary Crimes

ISBN/EAN: 9783337815950

Printed in Europe, USA, Canada, Australia, Japan

Cover: Foto ©Suzi / pixelio.de

More available books at **www.hansebooks.com**

BARBARA VILLIERS:

OR

A HISTORY OF MONETARY CRIMES.

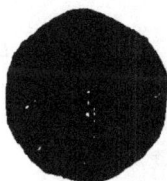

———

BY

ALEXANDER DEL MAR, M. E.

FORMERLY DIRECTOR OF THE BUREAU OF STATISTICS OF THE UNITED STATES
OF AMERICA; MINING COMMISSIONER TO THE UNITED STATES MONE-
TARY COMMISSION OF 1876; AUTHOR OF A "HISTORY OF
THE PRECIOUS METALS," "A HISTORY OF MONE-
TARY SYSTEMS," "THE SCIENCE OF MONEY,"
ETC., ETC.

OMNI PUBLICATIONS

Hawthorne, Calif. 90250

1983

First published ------1899

Library of Congress Catalog Card Number 67-28927

Printed in the United States of America

INTRODUCTION.

THE insidious crime of secretly or surreptitiously altering the monetary laws of a State—than which no more dastardly or fatal blow can be dealt at its liberties—is not a new one. There is a suggestion in the decree of B. C. 360, concerning the ancient iron money of Sparta, that Gylipus was not unfamiliar with this grave offence. In a later age, Pliny, who justly calls it "a crime against mankind," evidently refers to that alteration of the Roman mint code by which what remained of the nummulary system of the Republic was subverted, about B. C. 200, in favor of the authorised private coinages of the gentes. Such alteration seems to have been secret, for no explicit allusion to it appears in the fragments that have been preserved concerning the legislation of that period. But the coinages and the decadence of the State tell the story with sufficient distinctness to justify the anathema of the Roman encyclopedist.

Upon the establishment of the Empire, the State resumed the entire control of its monetary issues; and this policy it continued to maintain until the barbarian revolts of the fifth and sixth centuries subverted or weakened its authority and obliged it to connive at breaches of the prerogative which it had lost the power to prevent or punish. The latest notable exercise of its resentment for an usurpation of the coinage prerogative was the war which Justinian II. declared against Abd-el-Melik for daring to strike and issue gold coins without the Imperial stamp or authority.

After the Fall of Constantinople in 1204, the prerogative of the Roman Emperor fell into the hands of the numerous potentates who erected their crowns upon the ruins of the empire and its maintenance became the source of numerous contests with the inferior nobles, who, in their ignorance and avidity, would fain have retained a right. which, so long as it remained in their hands, rendered the erection of kingdoms and therefore the recognition and due support of their own nobility, impossible. The process of King Philip le Bel against the Comte de Nevers emphasised this view of the subject very clearly. Before the Discovery of America private coinage was everywhere suppressed; and the essential prerogative of Money became vested and centered in the various crowned heads who governed the states of Europe,

It was not long after that great event, when avidity awoke to new life over the spoils of a plundered Continent, that attempts were renewed to snatch the prerogative of Money from the State. This time it was not the truculent noble, who impudently claimed a right that had once belonged to the Cæsars and boldly exercised it in defiance of the Crown, but the sneaking billoneur, who stealthily sought to acquire it through the arts of falsehood, intrigue, and forgery.

Such were the crimes of 1666, 1742, 1870 and 1873.

LIST OF MR. DEL MAR'S WRITINGS.

I. *Gold Money and Paper Money*—New York, A. D. F. Randolph, 1862. Pamphlet.

II. *History and Principles of Taxation*—New York *Social Science Review*, 1865.

III. *Essays in Political Economy*—New York *Social Science Review*, 1866.

IV. *Statistics of the World*—Washington, Government Press, 1866. Pamphlet.

V. *What is Free Trade?*—New York; G. P. Putnam and Son, 1867. 12mo. 150 pp.

VI. *Decadence of American Shipbuilding*—Washington, Government Press, 1867. Pamphlet.

VII. *The Whiskey Tax for 100 Years*—Published by Congressional Sub-Committee on Retrenchment, 1868.

VIII. *Monthly Statistical Reports* on the Commerce, Navigation, Trade, Resources, &c., of the Various Countries of the World, from November, 1866, to January, 1869. Washington, Government Press. 26 vols. Quarto pamphlets.

IX. *Annual Reports on the Commerce and Navigation* of the United States of America, 1865, 1866, 1867, 1868. Washington, Government Press. 4 vols. 8vo. 700 to 800 pp. each.

X. *Operation of the Tariff Laws*—Familiarly known as the *Suppressed Report*. Washington, Government Press, 1868; Reprint, 1879.

XI. *Letter on the Finances*—New York; Douglass Taylor, 1868 Pamphlet.

XII. *Seven Essays on the Treasury*—New York; *Citizen* office. 1869. Pamphlets.

XIII. *Finances of the United States*—Columbus, Ohio, *Statesman* office, 1870. Pamphlet.

XIV. *Life Insurance for Women*—New York; *Underwriter* office, 1871.

XV. *History of the Rate of Interest*—New York; Proceedings of the National Insurance Convention, 1872. Pamphlet.

XVI. *Progress of Life Insurance*—St. Petersburgh; Imperial Press, 1872.

XVII. *A Summer Tour in High Latitudes, or Travels in Scandinavia, Finland, and Russia*—New York; *Appleton's Journal*, 1873.

XVIII. *Recollections of the Civil Service*—New York; *Appleton's Journal*, 1874.

XIX. *Agriculture of the World, by Countries*—Chicago *Times* and *Inter-Ocean*, 1874.

XX. *Resources of Egypt*—Philadelphia; McCalla and Staveley, 1874. Pamphlet.

XXI. *Resources of Spain*—Philadelphia; McCalla and Staveley, 1875. Pamphlet.

XXII. *Agriculture of Prussia*—New York; Wm. Barnes and Co., 1875. Pamphlet.

XXIII. *Productive Forces of Bavaria*—New York; Wm. Barnes and Co., 1875. Pamphlet.

XXIV. *Famishing Portugal*—Philadelphia; *Lippincott's Magazine*, 1876. Pamphlet.

XXV. *Production of Silver in the United States*—Washington, Government Press, 1876.

XXVI. *First List of all the Merchant Vessels* of the United States of America, with name, rig, tonnage, hailing port, and signal number of each one. Washington, Government Press, 1866 8vo., 300 pp.

XXVII   *Report on the Mines of the Comstock Lode*—Washington, Government Press, 1876.

XXVIII.   *Essays on the World's Production of Gold and Silver; Relative Value of Gold and Silver; Population and Money; Demonetization of Silver in Germany; The French War Indemnity: Movement of Silver to India; Metallic Standard of Money in the United States; Coinage of the United States; Metallic Standard of Money in the United Kingdom; Monetary System of Austria-Hungary,* and *Monetary System of China*—Printed in the Report of the U. S. Monetary Commission; Washington; Government Press, 1877.

XXIX.   *Real History of the Big Bonanza Mines*—San Francisco; Argonaut print, 1878.

XXX.   *Bill to Regulate Mining Companies*—Argument in California Senate Committee—Sacramento, 1878.   Pamphlet.

XXXI.   *Insanity and Crime in Mining Countries*—San Francisco; *Mining and Scientific Press*, 1878.

XXXII.   *Usury and the Jews*—San Francisco; I. N. Choynski, 1879.   Pamphlet.

XXXIII.   *Theory of Value*—San Francisco; *Mining and Scientific Press*, 1879.

XXXIV.   *The Principles of Insurance*—Argument in California Senate Committee on Corporations—San Francisco; Bosqui and Co., 1880.   Pamphlet.

XXXV.   *History of Money in China*—San Francisco; J. R. Brodie and Co., 1880.   Pamphlet.

XXXVI.   *History of the Precious Metals*—from the Earliest Times to the Present. London; Geo. Bell and Sons, 1880. 8vo., 373 pp.

XXXVII.   *Impeachment of the Treasury*—New York *Sun*, October, 1880.

XXXVIII.   *The Gold Drain and Impending Panic*—New York *Sun*, March 15th, 1884.

XXXIX.   *Rape of the Earth*—or Travels and Researches in the principal Mining Districts of North and South America, Europe, and Africa.   In Press.

XL.   *Essay on Corporations*—San Francisco; Printed by the Mechanics' Institute, 1884.   Pamphlet.

XLI.   *History of Money in Ancient Countries*—from the Earliest Times to the Present. London; Geo. Bell and Sons, 1885. 8vo., 400 pp.

XLII.   *The Science of Money.* London; Geo. Bell and Sons. 8vo., 124 pp.

XLIII.   *The Politics of Money.*

XLIV. *The Worship of Augustus Caesar*—Derived from a study of coins, monuments, calendars, aeras and astrological cycles, the whole establishing a New Chronology of History and Religion.

XLV.   *The Middle Ages Revisited* or the Roman Government and Religion from Augustus to the Fall of Constantinople.

XLVI.   *Ancient Britain* in the light of modern archaeological discoveries.

XLVII.   *History of Money in America*—From the Discovery, to the Foundation of the American Constitution.

XLVIII.   *Barbara Villiers*—A History of Monetary Crimes.

XLIX.   *The Beneficient Effects of Silver Money* during the 17th Century.

L.   *Money and Civilization*, 1885.

LI.   *Roman and Moslem Moneys.*

LII.   *History of Money in the Netherlands.*

BARBARA VILLIERS

OR A HISTORY OF

MONETARY CRIMES.

CHAPTER I.

THE CRIME OF 1666.

FROM the remotest time to the seventeenth century of our æra, the right to coin money and to regulate its value (by giving it denominations) and by limiting or increasing the quantity of it in circulation, was the exclusive prerogative of the State. In 1604, in the celebrated case of the Mixed Moneys,[1] this prerogative was affirmed under such extraordinary circumstances and with such an overwhelming array of judicial and forensic authority as to occasion alarm to the moneyed classes of England, who at once sought the means to overthrow it. These they found in the demands of the East India Company, the corruption of Parliament the profligacy of Charles II., and the influence of Barbara Villiers. The result was the surreptitious mint legislation of 1666-7: and thus a prerogative, which, next to the right of peace or war, is the most powerful instrument by which a State can influence the happiness of its subjects, was surrendered or sold for a song to a class of usurers, in whose hands it has remained ever since. In framing the American mint-laws of 1790-2, Mr. Hamilton, a young man (then 33 years of age), and wholly unaware of the character or bearings of this English legislation, innocently copied it and caused it to be incorporated in the laws of the United States, where it still remains, an obstacle to the equitable distribution of wealth and a menace to public prosperity.

More than this: down to the year 1870 the Crown of England had the right, without consulting Parliament, to undo much of the mis-

---

[1] A copious Digest of the "Mixed Moneys" case appears in the author's "Science of Money," chap. VII.

chief occasioned by the Act of 1666 and its logical sequel, the Act of 1816: that is to say, the Crown had the right and the power to restore the previous Monetary System of full legal tender gold and silver coins struck by the State for the convenience of the public and the benefit of trade; and not as now, merely upon the behest of the banking fraternity.   In that year this supernal power was surreptitiously filched from the prerogatives of the Crown.   The evil work was then carried to other countries especially to the United States of America, where in 1873 it was copied with a faithfulness to its model that could only have been born of design.

———

Upon the opening of trade with India in the 16th century a pound of gold metal could be exchanged or purchased in Asia for 6 to 8 pounds of silver metal, this being the ratio p..id for bullion at the Indian mints.   There was little or no silver in India; the natives of that country being ignorant of how to reduce argentiferous ores. Gold was comparatively plentiful, though it existed chiefly in the form of jewelry and other works of art.   The currency consisted mainly of copper and billon coins, with a comparatively few gold pieces, the latter being chiefly used in and about the courts of the reigning sovereigns and the great commercial cities.   Owing to these circumstances, the exchange of Western silver for Eastern gold became one of the chief sources of profit to Europeans engaged in the Oriental trade.   In 1542 the Spaniards commenced shipping silver to China and India, from Acapulco in Mexico, by way of the Phillpines.   When Potosí became prolific these shipments amounted to £200,000 a year.   By this time the value of a pound weight of gold in the coinages of India had been raised to 9 pounds weight of silver; in other words, the coinage ratio between silver and gold was 9 for 1.   The British East India Company, formed in 1600, at once sought permission from the Crown of England to export silver to India.   The policy of England had always been opposed to the melting or exportation of any portion of its Measure of Value.   Penal statutes, prohibiting such melting or exportation, had been enacted in 9 Edw'd III., c. 1.; 2 Hen. IV.,c. 5; 5 Rich. II.; 17 Rich. II.; 2 Hen. VI., c. 6; 17 Edward IV; 4 Hen. VII., c. 23; and 19 Hen. VII., c. 5.

Similar statutes were enacted by Henry II. and Henry V.   Such prohibition was still in force.   It embraced not only the coins of the realm but also those foreign coins, such as Spanish reals, to which the English laws had accorded currency, or legal-tender function, in

England at fixed prices in English money. In accordance with this policy, Queen Elizabeth refused the request of the Company, although it apparently related only to the Spanish coins then circulating in England. However, permission was given them to import new silver from foreign parts, which silver might then be struck into coins at the Mint for their special use (after due payment of seigniorage), with further permission to annually export a limited sum of the coins thus struck. The pieces fabricated under this ordnance are known as "portcullis" coins, from the figure stamped upon them. They were of the same weight, fineness and general design, as the Spanish dollars, halves and quarters of the period. This was in 1601; the coinage ratios at that time being 15 for 1 in England and 9 for 1 in India. At a somewhat later date, the Company exported uncurrent English coins, chiefly the testoons (shillings) and other base issues of Henry VIII. and Edward VI., which, though still legal tenders in Ireland, were decried in England and sold for old metal[1]. Such export, however, appears to have been without any express authority from the Government.

In 1613 the Company obtained a charter with extended powers; and its numbers, wealth and influence having greatly increased, it made several attempts to enlarge its privilege of export, one of which attempts was discussed in the Star Chamber, 1639, but without success to the Company. With the downfall of Charles I., the Company was almost extinguished. Its aggressiveness and avidity had procured it many enemies, and rendered it so unpopular that in 1655, Cromwell annulled its exclusive privileges and declared the Oriental trade open to all Englishmen. Two years later the Company's influence with the Council of State was sufficient to induce the Protector to renew its monopoly. In 1662 Charles II. confirmed this renewal and, for a corrupt consideration, permanently established this Company of money-changers, privateers, fillibusters and bullies. From that year dates a new order of men in England. The Estates formerly consisted of the Crown, the Church, the Lords and the Commons. To these were now added the financiers, or Billoneurs, who have since almost entirely swallowed the others. Originally the financiers consisted of 215 monopolists under the title of the East India Company: they now comprise the entire world of money-changers and bankers. This cosmopolitan band threatens the peace of mankind.

[1] Proceedings of the London Numismatic Society, April 25, 1895.

I propose in this treatise to relate at some length the history of their privileges and to indicate their mischievous influence.   There is romance in the history and profit in the moral.

CHAPTER II.

SILVER.

SILVER is rarely found in the form of metal, but chiefly as an ore, from which the metal is obtained by complicated processes. Nor is the ore usually found on or near the surface of the earth, but mostly in quartz veins, or in lodes and pockets which lie deeply buried in the recesses of metamorphic rocks. Hence silver was the last of the two great precious metals obtained by man; and it could not have been procured in any but minute quantities before the discovery of iron and the fabrication of iron and steel tools of sufficient hardness to cut the rocks in which silver ores are concealed. As for the suggestion that copper tools, hardened with tin, were sufficient for deep mining, we leave the inventors of this hypothesis to account for copper and tin metal themselves in any great quantity prior to the advent of steel tools.

The dependence of silver upon steel enables us to fix its æra with some degree of certainty. The Indian Brahmo-Buddhists, the Babylonians, Assyrians and Greeks all agreed in assigning the invention of iron and steel to about the beginning of the 14th Century B. C.

The Greek date was that of Jasius and the Ten Dactyles of Mount Ida, B. C., 1406. This date marks alike the æra of iron metal and of quartz mining; whether of gold, copper or silver[1].

The earliest use of silver for coins must be assigned to the East Indians, who, in their ramtenkis, or rama-tankas, employed a mixture of both gold and silver, called by the Greeks, electrum.

The earliest silver coins of the West were those of Pheidon, King of Argos, who, according to the Parian chronicle, struck them in the Isle of Ægina, near Athens, about B. C. 895, from silver, probably

---

[1] A fragment of Philo Byblius ascribes the invention of iron to "Chrysor, who is the same as Heph-æstus, Molech, or Zeus Meilikios or Meilichios. From him descended Taat, whom the Egyptians call Thoth and the Greeks Hermes" Milichius (the Holy) was a surname of Bacchus. "Phœnicia," p. 340: and Noel voc. "Milichius." Iasus, the discoverer of iron, was another name for Bacchus. Hence all these names referred to the same deity. According to Polydore Vergil, the discoverer of silver was Ericthonius of Athens. This is again the same divinity. The æra of this mythos was B. C. 1406.

obtained in the mines of Laurium The punched stater of Miletus,
now in the British museum, has been assigned upon artistic grounds
to the period B. C. 800, but Mionnet contends that it is not older
than Dàrius Histaspes. The electrum coins of Lydia are of a somewhat later date. The mines of Laurium were situated near Cape
Sunium, about 30 miles from Athens. The surface deposits probably
contained some native silver. There is reason to believe, from the
archaic remains found at Tiryns and their resemblance to those of
Byrsa (Carthage), that such surface deposits were originally worked
by the Phœnicians.

However this may be, the mines were certainly known to Æschy-
lus, Themistocles, Herodotus and other Greek writers of the fifth
and fourth centuries B. C., at which last named æra the excavations
were of some depth and the ores were of calamine and difficult to
reduce. In the time of Themistocles the annual produce of silver
amounted in value to that of the metal in about a million dollars of
the present day.

The systematic working of these mines marks an epoch in the history of silver. It gave rise to that rivalry for the trade of the Orient
which led to or kept up the wars between Greece and Persia.

Silver coins soon became common in all the Greek States; and
specimens of them are still extant. The ratio of weight in silver
and gold coins of the same value, at this period was, in India, 6 1-2
for 1, Persia 13 for 1 and Greece 10 for 1. In exchanging Western
silver for Indian gold the Persians made 100 per cent. and the
Greeks 50 per cent. profit.

The use of gold and silver coins was not universal in the Greek
States. The iron nummularies of Sparta under Lycurgus and the
nummulary system of Clazomenæ and Byzantium were remarkable
exceptions, which, in this place, can merely be mentioned, but
which nevertheless, especially the first one, deserve the careful ex-
amination of all students of money. They serve to prove, if nothing
more, that neither silver nor gold are indispensable for the purposes
of money or commerce. From a passage in Varro, preserved by
Charisius, viz., that "It is said that silver money was first made by
Servius Tullius," there is reason to believe that the Romans struck
silver coins at an earlier date than that mentioned by Pliny and that
silver and copper coins were used for money down to the period of the
Gaulish invasion. This system was abandoned, in A. U. 369 (B. C.
385), for a nummulary system consisting of highly overvalued bronze
counters, which formed the distinguishing money of the Republic,

until B. C. 316, when the plunder of Magna Graæcia led to the issue of the scrupulum coins of silver and gold at the weight ratio of 9 for 1. The capture of Tarentum in B. C. 271 led in B. C. 269 to a new coinage of silver and gold, this time at 10 for 1. Other coinages followed, which it is not deemed necessary to further mention in this place. In B. C. 206 Scipio Africanus conquered Spain for the Romans. Here began a new æra in the history of silver. Down to this time, indeed, until the Roman patricians acquired such command of the Statè and its possessions as to render them the arbiters of its destiny, the Republic controlled the issues of its mint and regulated, in the public interest, their number and value. From the moment that Spain fell to Scipio there arose a struggle among the priviledged class, to which that hero belonged, to control its silver mines and coinages.

The Iberian mines had been opened in ancient times by the Phœnicians and afterwards worked systematically by the Carthagenians. They were so numerous and prolific that historical writers have with one accord assigned to Spain during the Roman æra the same relative importance that is claimed for America during the 16th and 17th centuries. The control of the Spanish mines lawfully belonged to the Republic; but Strabo proved—and there are other evidences, derived from the appearance of the private coins, technically known as coins of the gentes—that shortly after the conquest of Spain the patricians of Rome acquired control of the silver mines and the privilege, under public regulation, of coining silver; the State still retaining and excercising the exclusive right to mine and coin gold.[4] The gentes coins were struck at the ratio of 10 silver to 1 gold, until the time of Sylla, when their weight was reduced, so that the ratio stood at 9 for 1, and this continued until the accession of Julius Cæsar, when private coinage and meltage was abolished and the ratio was raised to 12 for 1. It was during the period from Sylla to Cæsar when most of the gentes coins, now extant, were struck. The silver denarius of this period weighed 60.6 English grains. Of these, 25 were valued at one gold aureus of 168.3 grains. Hence $60.6 \times 25 = 1515 \div 168.3 = 9$; which was the ratio between silver and gold between B. C. 82 and B. C. 45.

From the accession of Cæsar, to the sixth century, the principal supplies of silver were obtained by the Romans in Spain, as elsewhere, by means of slave labor. These supplies were then materi-

4 Strabo, Geog. III., ii. 9.

ally lessened by the rising or invasion of the Visigoths, who, in remembrance of the cruelties suffered by their kinsmen under Roman masters, peremptorily closed the mines of Spain and forbade their being worked at all. The silver mines of Hungary, Bohemia, Germany, Gaul and Britain fell under the control of other "barbarians;" and though in the eighth century the Arabs conquered Spain and reopened its silver mines, the product did not go to Rome, but was employed in that new trade with the Orient which the Moslems and Goths had inaugurated. Substantially, from the sixth to the thirteenth centuries, the European supplies of silver went to the Moslem and Gothic traders, who swept the seas which encircle the Continent, and controlled the trades of the Levant, the Baltic, and the Orient. The weight ratio of value between the precious metals within the Roman Empire always remained where Cæsar fixed it, at 12 for 1; but the Moslems and Goths without the Roman Empire fixed it at 6 1-2 for 1, the same as it was in India. These two widely different ratios, the Roman and Indian, continued to antagonise one another in Europe, with more or less influence upon the coinages of those frontier states which did not fully fall within the sphere of either system, until the introduction of Christianity into the Gothic States and the decay of the Moslem power in Spain, when the Roman ratio of 12 for 1 again asserted its ascendency. This ascendency was, however, but temporary. Rome itself fell in •1204 (capture of Byzantium by the Latins and Venetians) and the coinage of gold, which, down to that time, had been exclusively exercised by the Roman (Byzantine) sovereign-pontiff—thus enabling him to keep the ratio unchanged—was usurped by every State that rose upon the ruins of the Empire. From the fall of Byzantium to the opening of Potosí in 1545 Europe witnessed every change in the relative value of silver and gold that provincial jealousy, avidity, expediency, or necessity could suggest.

For thirteen centuries the ratio within the Empire had remained steadily fixed at 12 for 1. During the following three centuries it varied in the coinage laws and coinage of Europe from 1 for 1 to 20 for 1. In 1535 the silver mines of Potosí were discovered; in 1545 these mines were opened systematically. In 1567 the "patio" process was discovered. From this period commenced that new and latest æra in the history of silver which it is the purpose of this work to illustrate. In 1591 the Spanish Viceroys in America were authorized to coin silver and to furnish such coins in exchange for silver bullion upon which the King's fifth, 20 per cent., and other dues, amounting to about 1 1-2 per cent. more, had been paid. In 1608 the Viceroys were instructed to coin for private account and free of charge all duty-paid silver brought to the Viceregal mints, except when regard for the public interest rendered it in their judgment more expedient to cease coinage. This was practically unrestricted and gratuitous, but not yet unlimited, coinage.

It is with this last mentioned subject that we shall presently have to deal. Meanwhile it is necessary to mention the quantitative influence of gold and silver and to briefly trace the history of coining by machinery.

In my article "Silver," in the Encyclopedia Britannica, 9th edition, signed "A. DE.," I said that "the greater rapidity with which gold can be obtained (as compared with silver) has often influenced the legal relation of value between these two metals." For example, when in 1668 the King of Portugal found that large supplies of gold were coming into his coffers from the Brazilian placers, he raised the mint price of gold from 13 1-3 silver to 16 silver. Hence the origin —for such was the origin—of this celebrated ratio was purely arbitrary and entirely opposed to the natural order of things. Silver did not fall owing to plentifulness, nor gold rise owing to scarcity. On the contrary, gold rose because the royal dues in that metal were so vast that the King of the principal coining country of that period deemed it worth while to raise its mint value in order to still further enhance the royal revenues. By the year 1747 the sporadic product of Brazil was substantially exhausted, and the King of Portugal, finding that his dues were now chiefly paid in silver, arbitrarily raised that metal from 16 to its former weight ratio of 13 1-3 for 1 of gold But at this period Portugal was ruined, and it did not much matter what the king did. The cause of her rise was the Plunder of the Orient and the Exploitation of the Brazilian placers; the cause of her fall was the sudden exhaustion of these sinister sources of wealth.

In all questions concerning coinage it must be borne in mind that gold has in fact been obtained chiefly from placers; that for the most part the placers needed no capital for their development, and that for this reason and also because placer gold is on or near the surface, the placers can be and always have been worked by a great number of people at once: hence that they can throw, and in fact have thrown, a vast quantity of metal upon the mints in a short space of time. It is no answer to these circumstances that the known placers are exhausted, or that there are no more placers to be discovered. Alaska is a recent and stubborn fact to the contrary; and until the entire earth, habitable or otherwise, is ransacked and washed over, the retention of gold as a Measure of Value exposes all the existing arrangements of men and things to disastrous revulsions.

Silver, on the contrary, is slow of production. The metal is locked up in the rocks, 28 cubic feet of which (mining "drives" or galleries are usually 7 feet high and 4 feet wide) have to be excavated in order to bring to the surface one lineal foot of vein matter, which is rarely more than a few feet thick. A silver mine needs capital and metallurgical skill for its development; while only a comparatively few men can work in one simultaneously.

For these reasons the production of silver has always been, and if not disturbed by legislation would always be, far more steady than that of gold. Its gradual demonetization is therefore without any apology either in the manner of its finding or production. As will be shown in the course of this work, it has been the result of intrigues which originated and have continued to emanate from the city of London, a place in which there are neither gold nor silver mines, but a plentiful accumulation of "financial" and commercial shrewdness. .

I would not have it inferred from these remarks that I prefer silver to gold for a general Measure of Value. A general or universal Measure of Value is a chimera invented by the bankers of Threadneedle Street to foist their Metallic scheme upon the world and render their city the centre of a system of cosmopolitan Barter. A national Measure of Value, consisting of silver metal ("free coinage" system), is but little better than one of gold metal. No metal, as such, can measure value with precision or equity. This is what Money alone can effect; and if there were no question of policy in the matter, I should advocate a monetary system independent of metals. But the monetary question is a practical and political one. We cannot ignore history; we cannot ignore the status quo; and as the status quo is a complex metal and paper system based upon history, law and practical politics, the most that can be done is to reform it in the interest of the government, that is to say, of the people. For the present I would advise a return to the coinage laws prior to 1873 and the retirement of bank notes, to be replaced by greenbacks. These reforms will not only benefit the great mass of our people, they will save the commercial classes from what will otherwise end in widespread bankruptcy and perhaps even more serious results.

Unfortunately the commercial classes are too greedy to accept reforms that do not promise them unfair advantages.

CHAPTER III.

THE COINING MILL AND PRESS.

THE quantity of silver produced by the mines of Potosí was so ample that when turned into money it promised to promote new currents of trade, new inventions and new enterprises and achievements of every description. European States had long been destitute of an adequate Measure of Value There were but few gold coins in circulation. The silver coins were mostly degraded. The monetary issues were chiefly billon and copper coins, whose value depended largely upon government credit, which at that period was much strained. The entire monetary circulation of Europe at the period of the Discovery of America did not exceed $2 per capita. Agriculture was degraded to the lowest condition; the peasantry were reduced to the level of animals; commerce and private credit had folded their wings and shrunk into the Italian ports; whilst manufactures, beyond a few homespun fabrics, had practically no existence. The desire to immediately convert the new supplies of silver into money was irresistible. By the hammer process an ordinary workman could not turn out more than forty or fifty well finished silver coins per diem and a good workman not more than a hundred. To coin the product of Potosí would have required an army of moneyers as numerous as those, whose revolt had cost the Emperor Aurelian 7000 troops to suppress. Something more expeditious was wanted than the old steel die, hammer and file. That something, in the shape of a laminating mill and screw coining press, the "balancier," was invented in Italy about the year 1547. It appeared in Spain in the year 1548. In 1550 some such a machine made its appearance in France, a country which possessed no Potosí and produced no silver. On March 3, 1553. a coin mill, the "lamanoir," was patented by Aubry Olivier. Another one was claimed as an invention of Antoine Brucher. [1] In July, 1553, the King, Henry II., of

---

[1] Benevenuto Cellini "Traité de l'orfévrerie," ch. ix: Renier Chalon, Hist. Fab. de Monnais; Henfrey, English Coins, p. 306, citing Le Blanc; Evelyn (" Medals," 225) relying upon Hierom Cardan, says that, Le Blanc to the contrary, notwithstanding, the Venetian Zeccha or mint, stamped, cut and rounded coins by one operation long before this was done in England and France: but the statement is not explicit enough to warrant any altertion of our text.

France, authorized the erection of a screw press and laminating mill
with which to coin silver testoons, or shillings. [6] In March, 1554,
the first coins, in France, were made by the new process. [7] In
1561 the mill-and-press was introduced by Nicholas Briot into
England. In 1685 Castaign invented a device to stamp the edges of
coins, and succeeded in turning out as many as twenty thousand .
coins a day by the new process. [8]

There are still extant some machine-made or "milled" coins of
Elizabeth, struck, according to Haydn, in the year 1562. Snelling
fixes the date of this event in 1576, but this seems to be too late;
for, according to Martin Folkes, Phillip Mastrelle, a Frenchman,
probably he who had brought the newest machine from France, was in
1569 detected in making coins on his own account, and for this offense
he was executed; a circumstance that put an end, for a time, to the
fabrication of coins by machinery in England. On the other hand,
Blackie's Popular Encyclopedia states that Mastrelle's press was not
abandoned until 1572. The true date of Mastrelle's death may
possibly be supplied by Fénélon, who states that in September, 1574,
certain Germans, Hollanders and Frenchmen, in England, were
detected in forging a million crowns of the coins of France, Spain
Flanders; and that this was done with the connivance of some of
Elizabeth's ministers. [9] So vast a number of broad pieces would
hardly have been attempted to be struck by hand; and since
Mastrelle, so far as is known, possessed the only complete coining
machinery in England, it seems more than likely, especially when
regard is had for Mr. Folkes' statement, that Fénélon's account is
correct and Mastrelle was either the instigator or chief instrument of
these nefarious transactions. Similar offenses were perpetrated in
France. The Marquis de Tavannes assures us that Salcede, who
was executed in 1582, had grown rich from the profits of what he
called forgery, but what, according to the Metallic school was really
only justifiable private coinage; because the forged coins contained
more silver than the genuine. It is evident that the mill-and-press
was already working a revolution in the monetary systems of the
world. So far as it operated to discourage the further issuance of
debased coins, like those, for example, of Edward VI., its influence

[6] Boisard, "Traite de Monnoyes," ed. 1714.
[7] Humphrey's "Coin Manual," p. 460, citing Folkes.
[8] Boisard I., 142; Penny Encyc.; Renier Chalon.
[9] "Money and Civilization," ch. X, citing Buckle's "Posthumous Works," and
Fénélon, VI., 241-2.

wàs admittedly beneficial. But might it not also operate to destroy money altogether, by facilitating its reduction to the degraded level and value of the metal of which it was made? We shall see.

It has been suggested by Blackie's Pop. Encyclo., (art. "Mint,") that Mastrelle's mill-and-press was abandoned in England in 1572, on account of the superior cheapness of fabricating coins by hand! A similar reason is advanced by Renier Chalon for the abandonment of the mill-and-press in France, by Henry III., in September, 1585. Aside from the improbability of such alleged cheapness, the executions of Mastrelle and Salcede sufficiently prove that the renunciation of the new machine had a graver object. This was to limit the coinage and discourage counterfeiting. But though it was comparatively easy to detect and drive forgers out of the well policed States of Europe, it was not so easy to discover and punish them in America. Counterfeit silver coins were reported in circulation and are mentioned in the Spanish-American monetary laws of 1535, 1565 and 1595, which contain injunctions to the Spanish viceroys to trace and punish the offenders.

In 1603 the billon coins of Phillip III., in Spain, like those of Henry VIII. and Edward VI. in England, were suddenly doubled in value by royal proclamation. The Spanish decree produced great distress and confusion. It was followed in Spain by a virtual suspension of payments in gold or silver coins and a premium on the latter of 40 per cent. in billon money. Worst than all, this ill-advised measure afforded not merely encouragement but protection to the Spanish-American counterfeiters of silver coins; for even the officers of government were indisposed to interfere with men who offered to them, in exchange for the debased coins of the Crown, the superior products of forgery. The consequence was that much of the newly-mined silver was enabled to avoid the production tax of a fifth (the Quinto), the forgers buying the metal secretly from the miners and working it into well-made coins of high standard, most of which found their way direct from America to the Orient, and some even to Europe. When the news of these events reached Spain the Crown took alarm; and for a ready way out of the many difficulties which beset the subject, it plunged into a new one, far worse than all the others: in 1608 it authorized its viceroys in America to freely coin all tax-paid silver. This was practically private and unlimited coinage; it also implied unlimited freedom to export and melt.

Between the first and third quarters of the 17th century the new

coining process passed through many experimental and probationary
stages. In 1617 one Balancier is said to have invented an improved
mill-and-screw. [10] In 1625 Nicholas Briot invented an improved
machine, and in 1631 he was invited or permitted by the Royal Mint
of England to manufacture coins in the Tower of London by means
of the new mill-and-screw; several issues of Charles I. affording
evidence of the fact. But owing to some misunderstanding, or perhaps by reason of the patronage which Louis XIII. extended to the
coining press and the more permanent, profitable, or congenial employment which awaited Briot in his own country, he returned to it
soon afterwards. In December, 1639, Louis XIII., of France, issued
an edict which authorized the manufacture of coins in the Royal
Mint by the new process. In March, 1640, he went still further: he
forbade the manufacture of hammered coins, unless the same were
finished as evenly and perfectly as those by the mill-and-screw,
which, of course, was practically impossible. [11] This encouragement of the new process was evidently offered as a remedy for the
evil effects of that picking out and secret melting down of the
heavier hammered coins (the crime of billonage) which half a century
later produced so much commotion in England and already began to
be felt in France. In 1645, third year of Louis XIV., all coinage
was forbidden except by the new processs, which now became permanently established in France, whereas in England it was still on
trial. [12]

In that country political disturbance had for a while postponed
definite action on this important subject. In 1651 Pierre Blondeau,
a Frenchman, was employed by the government of Oliver Cromwell
to strike coins by the mill-and-screw. His work, however, was confined to pattern pieces, [13] which, according to the Penny Cyclopedia,
were the first ones upon whose edges a lettering was impressed, as a
safeguard against clipping: the serrated edges not appearing until
1663. After some delays Pierre Blondeau in 1659 got to work systematically, [14] but here again political events occurred to interrupt
the employment of the new process. In 1660 the Restoration took
place; Blondeau was frightened back to his native land; and the
early coins of Charles II. were once more hammered, as of old. [15]

[10] Putnam's "Cyc. of Chron.," art. "Coining." The name Balancier suggests a
maker. The date is that of Briot's invention.
[11] Boisard. [12] Boisard, 108.
[13] Proc. Num. Soc., VI., 261. [14] Humphreys 474.
[15] Humphreys, 475.

But the time had passed for this ancient process. Milled and pressed coins were being produced in France, Holland and Spanish America, of so much more even weights and such superior workmanship, that England, unless content to let the Eastern trade slip into the hands of its neighbors, was compelled to adopt the new process, even though it became necessary to employ foreign artists to superintend the work. Accordingly Pierre Blondeau was sent for again; and the year 1662 saw him re-employed at the Tower of London, turning out with mill-and-screw those handsome coins upon which the restored but improvident Charles had already granted a mortgage to his beautiful Barbara Villiers. The superior results of machine coining are seen by a single glance at the statistics of the mint. From the Restoration (in May) to the end of the calendar year 1660, the coinage was only £1,683; in 1661, £23,200; in 1662, when Blondeau's machines were employed, £496,678; and in 1663, £330,507. Here Blondeau seems to have been dismissed, or else the supplies of bullion ran very low, for in the following three or four years the coinage did not average £50,000. Year 1664, £44,333; 1665, £61,722; 1666, £37,144; 1667, £53,106. Whether a French mintner was again employed or not, does not appear; but the increase of the coinage from 1668 onward unmistakedly indicates the permanent establishment of the new process. The year 1668, £124,940; 1669, £44,305; 1670, £143,043; 1671, £119,800; 1672, £268,688; 1673, £313,300.

In the previous chapter mention was made of the ancient statutes, which, in order to prevent any alteration in the Measure of Value, prohibited the melting down or exportation of the National coins. Down to Edward III. the statutes against melting related only to silver pennies, half-pennies and farthings; and from Edward III. to Richard II. only to pennies and their fractions and to groats and half-groats, the largest silver coins of the period. After Richard II. there was no new statute against melting, although there were several against exportation. The goldsmiths, bankers and foreign merchants of London, always conspicuous for their unselfish patriotism and devotion to the public interest, construed these statutes so literally a. to deem themselves at liberty to melt down all the broad pieces of Cromwell and the two Charleses, which had been so carefully minted by Briot and Blondeau; and to export the metal thus obtained to the Orient. A penal statute in 1662 was enacted to stop this practice, but it was followed so closely by the opposite legislation of 1663 and 1666, presently to be described, that it had no practical result. [16]

[16] Anderson, II., 465; Ruding II., 9.

As Mr. Davis, a member of Parliament in Elizabeth's reign, had said in reference to the same practice of exportation: "The exchange is governed by brokers and as it pleaseth them, the exchange must rise and fall"; which was as true in the reign of Charles as of Elizabeth; and is as true of the United States to-day as it was of England in the reign of Charles.

CHAPTER IV.

THE EAST INDIA COMPANY.

THUS far the monetary legislation of the 17th century related to a legal decision and to a mechanical invention by which coins could be manufactured of a uniform weight and size, a thing practically impossible by the process of hammering and hand-punching.

By the new invention coins could also be produced cheaply, so that small coins of silver, of billon and even of tin and copper, could be manufactured economically, rapidly and measuredly safe from the arts of forgers. Afterwards, the monetary legislation related to an intrigue which originated with the billoneurs, the goldsmiths or bankers and their commercial colleagues, namely, the 215 nobles, knights, aldermen and merchants, trading with the Indies, under the title of the East India Company. It was consummated under the auspices of the king's mistress, Barbara Villiers, Countess of Castlemaine, and afterwards Duchess of Cleveland. Finally, it fell alto-together under the influence of the all-absorbing East India Company.

By the charter granted to the East India Company, December 31, 1600, it was permitted to export foreign coin or bullion to the amount of £30,000 a year, upon condition that the Company imported within six months after the completion of every voyage, except the first one, the same quantity of foreign coin and bullion that it had exported. [17] It may here be stated that from the year 1600 the seigniorage on silver coins levied by Elizabeth was two shillings on 62 shillings, the coinage value of the pound weight of standard silver; by James I., two shillings-and-six pence; by Charles I. and the Commonwealth it was two shillings, [18] and by Charles II., until 1667, it was two shillings to the Crown and two pence to Barbara Villiers. [19] The privileges granted in 1600 to the East India Company were so lucrative that the restrictions which accompanied them had not yet produced dissatisfaction. The trade in general com-

[17] McCulloch, "Com. Dic.," p. 515. [18] Snelling's "Silver Coins."
[19] Act 18, Chas. II., ch. 5, paragraph 12.

modities was slow, hazardous, and comparatively small. After 1635 the Company was handicapped by the charter granted to Sir William Courten (the son of a thrifty tailor) and others, authorizing them to trade with those parts of India which the Company had neglected. In 1637 Courten's Company was granted further privileges, including that of exporting within five years not over £40,000 in coin and bullion to India. This practically meant silver coin or bullion; and it enabled the whole sum to be exported in one year. During the Commonwealth the operations of this rival association were conducted upon a scale of such magnitude and with such concessions to buyers that profits were reduced to a minimum, and the continuance of both the original British and Dutch East India Companies was seriously endangered. In this emergency the billoneurs and capitalists of Amsterdam and London took counsel of one another, and in 1649 succeeded in forming a union of the rival associations; after which prices and profits both took an upward turn. However, the union was not a lasting one. It had its disadvantages, and prominent among these were the restrictions placed upon the East India Company by the government of Elizabeth with regard to the export of coin and bullion. These restrictions were still, at least outwardly, observed by the Company, whereas Courten and his associates had never previous to the amalgamation deemed themselves bound to pay any respect to the like restrictions upon their Company. The latter, therefore, longed to be free. They represented to the Government, as indeed they had done several years previously, that the East India Company's charter legally expired with the death of Charles I; that the East India Company had in fact exceeded their privilege in the export of coin and bullion, and had thereby occasioned a great scarcity of silver coin in England; and that they had "neglected to establish fortified factories or seats of trade to which British subjects in the Orient could resort with safety."

In consequence of these specious representations, Cromwell, in 1655 proclaimed free trade to the Indies for three years; but he does not appear to have been satisfied with the results of the experiment; for in 1657 (February 10) the Council of State gave it as their advice to the Protector, "that the trade of East India be managed by a United Joint Stock, exclusive of all others." This led in the same year to a renewal of the envied charter to the East India Company. This charter was confirmed and the powers of the Company, except as to the export of coin and bullion, were greatly enlarged by Charles II., April 3, 1661.

In a work entitled "The Halcyon Age of the World" I have set forth the various expeditions, legal and illegal, which were organised in England and the West Indies during the 17th century to rob the Spaniards of the spoil which they had previously plundered from the natives of America. Hawkins, Drake, Frobisher, Morgan and many others had conducted these expeditions, whose fruit was chiefly the gold and silver which had been wrung from the blood and tears of the Indians. To convert this spoil into money was the first desire of the plunderers. The Buccaneers sold it at 10 per cent. discount to the illicit mint at Boston, Mass.; the pirates sold it to the fences in England at 25 per cent. off, and the privateers to the goldsmiths at 5 to 10 per cent. off. All these parties sighed for a purchaser who would buy without question every lot that was offered, pay for it in money containing precisely the same weight of pure metal, and place no restriction upon its exportation to India or elsewhere.

CHAPTER V.

BARBARA VILLIERS.

WE now come to the intrigue which was set afoot to remove this restriction, and to deprive the Crown of its seigniorage upon coins, but which, as it happened, had the far more important and lasting effect to substantially deprive the State of its control over the Measure of Value. This intrigue began directly after Blondeau was employed by Charles II. and had put his coining machines to work in the Tower. Its inceptors were the "goldsmiths" (or bankers) of Lombard Street; its instrument was a woman.

Barbara, the only child of William, viscount Grandison, was born in Ireland in 1640, and at the age of 16, being already famous for her extreme beauty and vivacity, was married to Sir Edward Villiers, who died in the following year. After the prescribed interval of mourning the young woman married the rich Roger Palmer, who in 1661, that is to say, a year after Barbara had become the king's mistress, was rewarded for his complaisance with the title of the Earl of Castlemaine. Pepys tersely describes Barbara as a "pretty woman . . . her husband a cuckold," and says that she turned papist not for conscience sake, but to please the king. He adds that the news of her "conversion," in 1663, was carried to Bishop Stillingfleet by William Penn, the Quaker.

The relations between the king and Barbara Villiers, then Mrs. Palmer, began on the very first day of the Restoration,[90] May 21, 1660. The woman was both depraved and sordid, and she seized upon every occasion to augment her power and fill her purse. She afterwards had, or was reproached with having had, intrigues with Mr. Rowly, Lord Chesterfield, Mr. Churchills, Harry Jermin (Lord Dover), Charles Hart, Jacob Hall, "Fleshy Will of Market Clare," Mr. Goodman, Robert ("Beau") Fielding, Ralph, Duke of Montague, the Viscount Chateillun, and others.[91] Defoe afterwards maliciously

[90] Bishop Burnett's " History of His Own Times," I., 160.
[91] Harris's " Life of Charles II.," vol. II., p. 293.

remarked that Charles II. had by his own efforts contributed four dukes to the peerage, alluding by this to the dukes of Grafton, Richmond, St. Albans and Buccleugh." But if the stories of Barbara's numerous intrigues had any foundation in fact, Defoe missed his mark by shooting too low.

With Barbara's subsequent marriage to and divorce from Fielding, in 1705-7, this treatise has no concern. Evelyn described her as a "lady of pleasure and the curse of our nation." " Pepys alludes to her as "a burden and reproach" to the country. " Clarendon said she would sell everything in the kingdom. " She was supported by a vile faction, which included the Duke of Buckingham, Lord Ashley, Lord Arlington (Sir William Bennett), Sir William Coventry, and many others, five of whom afterwards constituted the notorious "Cabal" Ministry of 1670. Three months after her relations began with the king, to wit, on the 20th of August, 1660, she was granted by letters patent, a mortgage upon, or pension from, the mint, of "two pence by tale out of every pound weight troy of silver money-which should thenceforth be coined by virtue of any warrant or indenture made and to be made by his Majesty, his heirs, and successors from the 9th of August, 1660, for 21 years." By letters patent dated 19th January, 1664, she was granted £4,700 a year out of the Post Office revenues. " Besides these, she had several other pensions, and was concerned in the promotion of numerous grants, monopolies, benefices, and other sources of revenue. She won £25,000 on cards in a single night; in another, she lost £15,000, and would play for £1,000 to £1,500 upon the single cast of a die. " On one occasion the king paid £30,000 to clear her debts. "

The movement, which culminated in the Coinage Act of 1666, though it apparently originated with the East India Company, had long been supported by the landlord class, whose interest had caused them to view with alarm the influx of the precious metals from America which began with Potosí. According to Brantome, the fears of the French landlords from this source had amounted almost to phrensy. The Marquis de Tavannes even proposed to demonetise

" I am informed that it was the son and heir of this Duke of Buccleugh, for whom Adam Smith wrote that Treatise on the Wealth of Nations, whose sophistical chapter on Money still influences the policy of England and America.

" Evelyn's "Diary," II., 57.   " Pepy's "Diary," IV., 184.

" Steinman,92.

" "Case of Her Grace, the Dutchess of Cleveland," pamphlet.

" Steinmann, 100   " Steinmann, 79.

both the precious metals, and employ in their stead coins made of iron; in other words, of some substance that capital could control. Pending this proposal the creditor class in France tried to exact payments in écus and other special kinds of coins, which they hoped to render scarce by limiting or obstructing their coinage; but this plan was defeated by Henry II., who, in a public ordinance dated 1551, threatened with death any one who should attempt to thus defeat the beneficent influence of an increase of money. The English nobles, more fruitful in financial resource than their French compeers, devised another plan to check the rise of prices. This was to obtain permission, directly or indirectly, to melt the coins of the realm into plate, to export it to the Antipodes, to get rid of it in some way or another, and thus contract the Measure of Value. All that was needed was a repeal of the statutes against exporting and melting. A movement of this character was made, as previously stated, in the reign of Charles I., about the year 1639. The establishment of the Commonwealth postponed the accomplishment of the design, but no sooner did the Restoration occur than it was again taken up and pursued through the agency of the East India Company and Barbara Villiers.

CHAPTER VI.

THE CATTLE AND COINAGE BILL.

LET us commence with 1663. The object of the East India
Company, their backers the landlords of England, their colleagues the goldsmiths of London, and their agents in Parliament,
assisted by the Countess of Castlemaine's faction, was first, to remove
the restriction upon the exportation of coins and bullion; second, to
get rid of the State seigniorage upon the coins; and third, to usurp
the prerogative of coinage for themselves. These objects they
accomplished by means of separate measures. And here it is to be
noticed that the Mint laws of 1816 and 1870 in England and of 1873
in the United States of America, were likewise altered by means of
separate measures. By this device the extent and importance of the
alteration escaped attention.

I. The first measure of 1663 was entitled "An Act for the Encouragement of Trade." It provided that between the 1st of July and
the 20th of December in any year, all cattle imported from Ireland,
Wales or Scotland into England shall pay a duty of 20 shillings per
head [19]; and it repealed the various provisions that had theretofore
been enacted forbidding the export of coin or bullion from the
kingdom. The patriotic pretext for the first provision was that Irish
(and Scotch) cattle, already fattened, were imported into England
to the injury of English landlords, who were thus deprived of the
means of letting their pastures to advantage. The pretext for the
second provision was that trade generally was hindered by the restriction on the export of coin. On July 21, 1663, the bill, having
passed through the Commons, apparently without debate, and being
then on its third reading in the Lords, a protest against its enactment was signed by the Earl of Anglesey, for himself and others,
and delivered to the Commons. [20] Among other objections the Earl
of Anglesey urged the following:

---

[19] Anderson's "Hist. Com.," II, 477.
[20] "The Troubles of Ireland," by Arthur Annesley, Earl of Anglesey.

"There appearing already great want of money in His Majesty's
dominions and almost all the gold of His Majesty's stamp gone, notwithstanding the restraint made by law . . . it must necessarily
follow by this free exportation" (the balance of trade being against
us) "that our silver will also be carried away into foreign parts and all
trade fail for the want of money, *which is the Measure of it.*" . . . "It
trencheth highly upon the king's prerogative, he being by law the
only exchanger of money, and his interest (as) equal to command
that, as to command the militia of the kingdom, which cannot sub-
sist without it; and *it is dangerous to the peace of the kingdom when it
shall be in the power of half-a-dozen or half-a-score of rich, discontented,
or factious persons to make a bank (meaning an accumulation) of our
coin and bullion beyond the seas, for any mischief (this meant India) and
leave us in want of money when it shall not be in the king's power to
prevent it,* (the liberty being given by a law) nor to keep his mint
going—because money will yield more from, than at, the Mint . . .
Because a law of so great change and threatening so much danger is
made perpetual and not probationary." [11]

This nobleman, whose earnest patriotism appears in all his writings
and public actions, clearly perceived what the intriguants were
driving at, and plainly pointed out the unconstitutionality and mischievous effects of their bill; but without avail. There was no power
to which appeal could be made. The king was a voluptuary, a profli-
gate, the prey of panders and parasites. The people had been
silenced; the press was without influence; the Commons were in the
pockets of the East India Company; and the Lords were, many of
them, suitors at the palace for the forfeited estates, titles, benefices,
monopolies and privileges which the king squandered, or his favorites offered for sale. [12]

The corrupt character of the Cattle and Coinage Bill is indicated
by the indecent haste and urgency which were manifested in the
Lords to pass it. The Duke of Buckingham (a relative of Barbara
Villiers), who usually did not rise until eleven o'clock in the
morning, was now at his post at the opening of each session and
remained to the last; "and it grew quickly evident that there were
other reasons which caused so earnest a prosecution of it above the
encouragement of the breed of cattle in England, insomuch as the
Lord Ashley, who, next the Duke, (of Buckingham) appeared to be

---

[11] Cobbett's "Parliamentary History," IV, 283.

[12] "State of the Kingdom," written by the Earl of Anglesey in 1682, and first
published by Sir John Thompson in 1694.

the most violent supporter of the bill, could not forbear to urge it as an argument for the prosecuting it, that if this bill did not pass, all the rents in Ireland would rise," etc. "The whole debate upon the bill was so disorderly and unparliamentary that the like had never been before; no rules or orders of the House for the course and method of the debate were observed." The members of the corrupt faction spoke out of their turn and more often than they had a right to speak, and this gave rise to many violent scenes. "In fine there grew so great a license of words in this debate, and so many personal reflections that every day some quarrels arose to the great scandal and dishonor of a Court that was the supreme judicatory of the kingdom. "Buckingham was challenged to mortal combat by Lord Ossory, and after escaping this danger by skulking the meeting and charging his opponent in the House with having delivered an unlawful challenge to him, was assaulted with blows by the indignant Marquis of Dorchester."

In spite of all this and of many conferences between the Lords and Commons, whose obstinacy refused all accommodation or compromise, the bill was passed, after "Berwick-on-Tweed" was substituted for "Scotland" and the word "foreign" was prefixed to "coin and bullion." This measure appears in the Statute Book as the 15 Charles II., c. 7. ⁱⁱ The preamble to the coinage provision is in the following words:

§ XII. *Whereas,* "Several considerable and advantageous trades cannot be conveniently driven and carried on without the species of money or bullion, and that it is found by experience that they are carried in greatest abundance (as to a common market) to such places as give free liberty for exporting the same, and the better to keep in and increase the current coins of this kingdom"—therefore let us resolve to let them freely go out! In other words, after August 1, 1663, leave is given to export all foreign coins or bullion of gold or silver, free of interdict, regulation, or duties of any kind.

Another preamble occurs in § V to the effect that in order to keep the colonies in America and elsewhere in firmer dependence upon England, be it enacted (in §§ VI to XI) that henceforth all trade to and from such colonies may be conducted only in British ships, belonging, of course, though this is not mentioned in the act, to the East India Company, or their coadjutors, who sought, promoted or assisted in the enactment of these mischievous measures.

ⁱⁱ Clarendon's "Life," 375.   ⁱ⁴ Statutes, VIII, 160.

In every instance, whether the legislation related to the fattening of cattle or the export of coin, or the colonial trade, patriotic reasons were alleged as the motive; in every instance, the real motive was a corrupt and selfish one.

The export of coin was solely for the benefit of the East India Company, whose active member and clever apologist was Sir Josiah Child. This arch intriguant succeeded in getting many of his co-partners (now numbering 556) returned as members of the Commons, and, as we shall presently see, he kept a guilty hold upon them and others. The Irish Cattle Clause was a palpable bribe to the English landed interest in the House of Lords; whilst the Colonial Clause prevented the Americans from participating in the Oriental trade, and at the same time sufficed to appease those British ship-owners who did not enjoy the advantage of being shareholders in the East India Company. The moral status of Parliament at this period may be gathered from the fact that on July 27, 1663, a bill for the better observance of the Sabbath (probably closing the public-houses and restricting the liquor traffic), which bill had been enacted and was ready for the Royal assent, was "lost off the table of the House of Lords;" and on May 13, 1664, Mr. Brynne was censured in the House for "altering the draft of a bill relating to public-houses." [15] But there is more to be said on this subject as we proceed.

The immediate effect of the export-of-coin measure was to increase at a single bound the exports of silver coin, from England to the Orient, from £40,000 or £50,000, to £400,000, or £500,000 per annum. [16] Pollexfen says £40,000 increased to £600,000. [17]

Its further effects, the scarcity of coin in England, the clipping of the hammered coin, and the great recoinage of 1696 [18] are eloquently set forth by Macaulay, who, however, has entirely overlooked the source of all this mischief. While the act confined the exportation permit to foreign coin and bullion, it practically also permitted the exportation of English coin. All that was necessary was to melt the latter to bullion, which thus, it was argued, became foreign bullion, for it had originally come from Spanish America. In fact and apart from this subterfuge, there are practically no means to distinguish the nationality or origin of an ingot of gold or silver metal. Under

---

[15] "Parliamentary History," IV, 286, 292.

[16] Snelling's "Silver Coins," 46, note.   [17] Anderson's "Hist. Com.," II, 476.

[18] Anderson, sub anno, estimates it at 16 millions sterling and says it first gave occasion for the issue of Exchequer Bills. They were of £5 and £10 each and circulated as money.

these circumstances, the best of the foreign and English silver coins, the broad pieces of Spain and the milled coins of England, were melted down and shipped to India by Sir Josiah Child and his patriotic associates, and there exchanged for their own private benefit, for gold bullion at 9 to 10 for 1.

II. The next step of the Company was to obtain control of the Royal Prerogative of coinage and erect a mint of their own. By these means they would become the exchangers and coiners, not merely of the bullion which passed through Madras and the ports which had beeen opened to them, but through all the ports of India. At the same time it was not desirable to quite destroy the Royal Prerogative, for fear that distant and unlawful mints, like that of John Hull, in Boston, Massachusetts, might cease to confine their issues to local coins and extend them to others destined for the profitable trade of India. " To prevent this calamity, the Royal Prerogative was kept nominally alive, while, so far as the East India Company and the moneyed classes were concerned, not a vestige of it was permitted to remain.

" The Massachusetts " Pine Tree " shillings were struck during the thirty years, 1651-81. They contained 60 grains of silver, 0.925 fine. Snelling says the seigniorage was 5 per cent; Hutchinson says 6 1-2 per cent.

CHAPTER VII.

SURRENDER OF THE COINAGE PREROGATIVE.

THIS brings us to the coinage legislation of 1666-7. [40] Some twenty years after the Company had obtained from Elizabeth the privilege to export £30,000 a year in portcullis coins, Mr. Francis Day, one of the Company's agents, purchased a concession from the Rajah of Madras to strike "Three-swamy," or Lakshmi pagodas of gold at their factory and fort of St. George. Lakshmi was the wife of Ieshna or Vishnu. She was the mother of gods, the Indian Maia, Ceres, or Venus, the personification of maternity, abundance and increase. The Hindu Rajah who permitted the English merchants to strike these coins, was, no doubt, persuaded that they would be better or more economically and numerously fabricated than with the rude appliances of the native mintners; and that therefore the venerated image which they bore would be circulated far and wide. What the accommodating English merchants really designed was that they should go into the melting-pots of Europe; and this design was fully carried out. In 1661 Charles II. obtained, as part of the dowry of Catherine of Braganza, sister of Alfonso VI., King of Portugal, the island and city of Bombay, [41] which down to that year had belonged to the Crown of Portugal. In 1665 (Articles of January 14) it was taken possession of by the British Crown. On March 27, 1668, it was sold by Charles to the East India Company, together with all political powers necessary to its maintenance and defence, with the exception of the factory and fort of St. George at Madras. This was the beginning of the territorial possessions of the East India Company. It thus acquired the elements of a State; land, a people, certain political powers, and an army and navy. But one thing more was needed to complete its sovereignty: the power to coin, to evaluate by denominations and to circulate, money. This

---

[40] Until 1752, the official year, as with the Romans, began on 1st March. Brady, I., 64; Haydn, voc. "Year," says 25th March, This is still the official year. The coinage bill was passed in February 1666-7.

[41] Bombay is a Portuguese name, derived from Bombahia, or Fine Bay.

had been the object of the Act under consideration, which was put upon its passage shortly after Bombay was acquired by the Crown and when the Company fully expected to obtain that place from the complaisant Charles. Any open attempt to wrest the coining power from the Crown of England would have met with the resistance of a nation always jealous of its political rights. No Englishman would have listened to the proposal for a moment. But openness was not the Company's mode of procedure. Rather was it subterfuge and bribery. It first secured the influence of the Speaker and euphemistically entitled the bill, which under his auspices was introduced to the House of Commons, "An Act for the Encouragement of Coinage." In the speech to the king made by the Speaker, this pliant official referred to the scarcity of coin, which, as compared with the period preceeding the Commonwealth, had made itself generally apparent, by saying that: "We find your Majesty's mint not so well employed as formerly; and the reason is because the fees and wages of the officers and workmen is in part paid out of the bullion that is brought to be coined, and what is wanting is made up by your Majesty. We have, therefore, for the ease of your Majesty, and those that bring in any plate or bullion to be coined there, made another provision, by an imposition upon wines, brandy, and cyder imported from any foreign nations." [41]

The argument to the king was, in plain language, as follows: "As compared with the Elizabethan æra, there is a scarcity of coin in the kingdom. This is probably due at bottom to the amelioration by the Spanish Crown in 1608 of the previously heavy seigniorage levied upon the coinage of silver in Spanish America, and by a similar amelioration in the United Provinces of the Netherlands. It is due immediately to the unwillingness of our mintners to employ the new mill-and-screw process, by which, so recently as four years ago, a mintner in a given interval could strike twenty or more times as much money as now. But as our London merchants in their wisdom choose to attribute the scarcity of coin to the very moderate seigniorage levied by your Majesty, and especially to that surcharge of twopence in the pound tale of silver imposed for the benefit of your mistress, Barbara Villiers, which has occasioned great scandal and dissatisfaction, we propose to remedy the matter by taxing ourselves, your always loyal commoners, in paying a duty upon all future importations of spirits, wines, beer, cyder and vinegar, and by abolishing

[41] "Parliamentary History," IV, 355.

the seigniorage altogether.   As the existing seigniorage, grievous
as it appears to our London merchants, (especially of the East India
Company) does not in fact pay the expenses of your Majesty's mint,
this duty upon spirits, etc., will ease your Majesty of the deficit
which now you are obliged to make good, and at the same time—as
you will observe in Section XII—it will provide a sure annuity of
£600 a year which your Majesty will be enabled to settle upon
Barbara, in place of that precarious one hitherto afforded her by the
comparative inactivity of the mint.   Thus all parties will be gratified,
and we, your loyal commoners, the only losers.   The scarcity of coin
will be remedied, bullion in vast quantities will flow into the mint,
the merchants will rejoice, the phrase 'free coinage' will tickle the
ears of a people yearning for freedom of any sort, the duties on
liquors will please the already established publicans aud brewers,
your Majesty will be relieved of expense and Barbara will not only
be provided for, but what is perhaps still more desirable, (now that
you have other beauties in view), it will place her annuity entirely in
your Majesty's power, which now is a public charge and cannot be
withdrawn or withheld without the open and discreditable repudiation of a royal grant.   Upon our shoulders alone will the extra burden fall.   We shall bear it willingly, both as a proof of our profound
attachment to your Majesty's person, and because it complies with
the desire of that noble and unselfish body of London merchants,
goldsmiths, and dealers in money, whose prosperity is ever synony-
mous with that of the kingdom."

Through the united influence of the various parties who expected
to profit by this measure, and aided by the bribes of the East India
Company, this iniquitous and mischievous bill was got through Parliament and obtained the royal assent.   It swept away not only the
seigniorage of the Crown, but also its control over the issuance of
money, because it left this to the volition and pleasure of those who
choosed to bring metal to the mint to be coined, and these were
practically the East India Company and the goldsmith class, with
which it co-operated and which it influenced.   By a rule of the coinage which was afrerwards made, refusing any but large deposits of
bullion (the limit is now £10,000) the general public was virtually
shut out from the mint, which was thus fully subjected to the control
of the intriguants.

Judging from the remarks of the Speaker quoted above, as of the
date of January, 1667, the Act 18, Charles II., c. 5, was retroactive;
for in clause I it is made to operate from December 20, 1666, for five

years, and "until the end of the first session of Parliament then next following and no longer." It was really passed in January or February, 1667, probably the latter, and with certain unessential modifications was kept in force by 25 Charles II., c. 8, and by subsequent enactments down to 9 George III., c. 25 (year 1768), when it was made perpetual. [42] By a subsequent enactment, 38 George III., c. 59 (year 1798), the gratuitous and unlimited coinage of silver, at the request of private individuals, was restricted. By 56 George III., c. 68 (year 1816), it was suspended; and in 1870 it was abolished altogether; but it has been continued as to gold down to the present time. [44]

The act of 1666 entirely failed to realise any of the expectations that were held out in its title or preamble. It did not increase the coin of the kingdom, but on the contrary, diminished it. It did not ease the king, but on the contrary, robbed the State of its prerogative of coinage and the profits it would have made by the Indian exchange; it did not promote the trade and commerce of the kingdom, but only that of the East India Company. It did not even answer the expectations of Barbara Villiers, through whose influence, more than any other, it owed its success in the Lords; for she was soon after supplanted in the king's affections by the Duchess of Richmond, and she (Barbara) thrown aside as a broken toy. To everybody but the East India Company the bill was deceptive and injurious. It was engendered by avidity, spawned in corruption, and has worked nothing but mischief down to the present moment.

In the House of Lords, February 22, 1670, Lord Lucas declared that this bill had promoted a further scarcity of money. [45] Sir Dudley North was even more emphatic. He was "infinitely scandalised at the folly of this law, which made bullion and coined money par; so that any man might gain by melting; as, when the price of bullion riseth, a crown (5 shillings) shall melt into five shillings-and-sixpence; but on the other side, nothing could even be lost by coining; for, upon a glut of bullion he might get that way too, and upon a scarcity, melt again; and no kind of advantage by increase of money, as was pretended, like to come out."

[43] This was two years after the battle of Plassey and the introduction of a silver monetary system into India by the East India Company to supplant the gold and billon currency of the Moguls.

[44] Report and Papers relating to the International Monetary Conference, held in Paris, 1879. Appendix, pp. 309, et seq.

[45] "History of Parliament," second reading to Subsidy Bill.

The Lord Treasurer gave some of the banker-goldsmiths and Sir Dudley North a meeting. "Charles Duncombe, *a great advancer*, had *whispered somewhat in his lordship's ear*, that made him inclinable to the bill. Sir Dudley North reasoned with him against it, beyond · reply, and then the argument was: 'Let there be money, my Lord; by God, let there be money!' The reasons why this scheme prevailed were first that the Crown got by the coinage duty, to wit, the imposts on spirits, wines, beer, etc., out of which was to be paid the substitute annuity to Barbara Villiers; next, that the goldsmiths, who gained by the melting trade, were *advancers* to the Treasury and its favorites. The country gentlemen are commonly full of one profound mistake: which is, that if a great deal of money be made, they must, of course, have a share of it; such being the supposed consequence of what they call plenty of money. So little do assemblies of men follow the truth of things in their deliberations, but shallow unthought prejudices carry them away by shoals. In short, the bill passed, and the effects of it have been enough seen and felt; however, the evil has since been, somewhat, but not wholly, remedied." [46]

I am quite at a loss to imagine in what manner this evil hath since been remedied, either wholly or partly. On the contrary, the mischievous influence of this measure continually augments as time advances. The Rev. Dr. Ruding, in his "Annals of the Coinage," written during the early part of the present century, than whom no more cautious, impartial, nor competent authority could be cited, says in reference to this bill: "Its influence has been most fatal to the mint." [47] Said J. R. McCulloch, writing in 1844: "Down to 1666 a seigniorage or duty upon the coinage was usually charged upon the gold and silver coins issued by the mint; and it may be easily shown that the imposition of such a duty, when it is not carried to an undue height, is advantageous. A coin is more useful than a piece of uncoined bullion of the same weight and purity; the coinage fitting it to be used as money, while it does not unfit it to be used for any other purpose. When, therefore, a duty of seigniorage is laid upon coin, equal to the expense of coinage, it circulates at its real value; but when this charge is defrayed by the public, it circulates at less than its real value, and is consequently either melted down or exported whenever there is any demand for bullion in the arts, or any fall in the exchange." [48]

[46] "Life of Sir Dudley North," p. 79.
[47] Ruding, II, 12. See Harry Pollexfen's criticism on this Act.
[48] McCullough's "Commercial Dictionary," ed. 1844, p. 305.

But neither North, Ruding, nor McCulloch saw the whole of the mischievous influence of this legislation, because at the time that they wrote (previous to the demonetization of silver), these influences were not fully developed. We now perceive that these eminent authorities omitted the consideration of a circumstance invested with the profoundest importance. It has become a widespread belief that a coin, for example, a sovereign or a dollar, is merely a piece of metal whose value is determined by its weight and fineness, which weight and fineness is certified by the State, and that this is all that is effected by such stamp or seal of the State. So far is this from being true that were the State to fabricate two kinds of coins of precisely the same weight and fineness, on one of which is stamped: "This piece contains 25.8 grains of gold 0.9 fine," and on the other merely: "This piece is one dollar," I venture to say that, with open mints for the former, and all other mint laws swept away, the latter would command a premium of at least twenty per cent. With the mints closed to coinage for private individuals such premium would rise to 50, 100, possibly to several hundred per cent. Such is the superiority of legal tenders over mere bits of metal; such the value of government seal and endorsement; such the measure of the gratuity which by this mischievous law the government confers not upon the industrious miner or producer, but upon the idle speculator in bullion and exchange.

This law, which deprives the government of seigniorage, throws upon it the whole burden and expense of coinage; the maintenance of the mints and mint officers; the cost of watching, detecting, arresting and punishing counterfeiters; the loss of metal in smelting and refining; the loss by robbery and defalcation; and finally, the loss occasioned by the wear and tear of coins. These various items in the United States amount to several millions a year. They should properly come out of the coins, because they are all sustained for the benefit of the coins. A charge of "retinue," or "brassage" should cover the cost of fabrication and maintenance of the mints; while the superior value imparted to the metal by the imposition of the government stamp, should be compensated by a seigniorage. Such charges were common to all mints previous to the plunder of America and ascendancy of the goldsmith class. They were then swept away for the benefit of Barbara Villiers, the East India Company, and the community of billoneurs.

Here I am tempted to narrate a story concerning that illicit mint in Boston which afterwards gave rise to so much irritation between the British government and the New England colonists that became one of the causes which led to the Revolution. Charles II., upon being shown one of the Pine-tree shillings struck by this mint, became greatly offended at the assump- tion of the coinage prerogative by the Americans, a prerogative which, it must be remembered, he had already sold to the East India Company. He told Sir Thomas Temple that he would make the Americans rue the day when they had dared usurp the royal preroga- tive of coinage; but being informed that the Tree which appeared upon the coins was intended for the Royal Oak that had sheltered him in the days of his distress, he relented; and declaring that the American colonists were "honest dogs," he spared his distant thunder. [49]

[49] Humphreys, p. 478.

CHAPTER VIII.

BRIBERY AND CORRUPTION.

IT is now in order to review the operations of the East India Company with reference to the coinage and to weigh the evidences concerning the means which they emyloyed to procure the passage of the act of 1666-7. As before stated, the Company acquired Bombay in 1668. Two years afterwards (1670) the Cabal Ministry was formed, and one year later (1671), the Company erected a mint in Bombay. [10] This was the same year, January, 1671-2, in which Charles II., after having solemnly assured the merchants of London that their deposits in the Royal Exchequer were perfectly safe and inviolable, coolly robbed them of the whole amount, about £1,328,526, and closed the Exchequer to further demands. Perhaps he had by this time discovered how the Crown had been cheated by the Act of 1666-7, and deemed himself justified in making reprisals from the class that had deceived him. But unfortunately, financial reprisals more often injure the innocent than the guilty. In getting even with the goldsmiths, Charles ruined ten thousand private families, innocent of crime against either him or the State. [11]

By its fourth charter, dated October 5, 1677, the East India Company was authorized by the Crown to coin in India and with its own stamp, both gold, silver, copper, and lead. [12] During the fifteen years which followed this grant, the Company must have transported from Europe to the Orient and there exchanged for gold, or for East India goods at Oriental gold prices, something like £7,500,000 in silver. If to this is added £40,000 a year from 1601 to 1666 and £400,000 a year from 1666 to 1677, the grand total of silver exported

---

[10] The Cabal Ministry consisted of Sir Thomas, afterwards Lord Clifford (C.), Lord Ashley (A.), afterwards Earl of Shaftesbury, George Villiers, Duke of Buchingham (B.), Henry Bennet, afterwards Earl of Arlington, (A.), and John Maitland, who was also Lord Thirlestane and Earl of Lauderdale (L.). Most of these men were concealed papists; Bennet's daughter was married to the Duke of Grafton, one of Barbara Villiers' sons.

[11] Anderson, II, 519; Sinclair's "Hist. Br. Rev.," 396. His father, Charles I., had previously (in 1638) robbed the Treasury of £200,000. Anderson, II, 386.

[12] Del Mar's "Hist. Monetary Systems," 474.

by this Company to the Orient, down to the beginning of 1693, could scarcely have fallen short of £15,000,000, upon which it secured an average profit, after all expenses and losses were paid, of not less than one third, or say £5,000,000. I am aware that, according to the accounts presented by the Company to Parliament, the exports of coin and bullion to India were much less, " but in the first place, these statistics only cover "India," not the Orient generally, and in the second place, they are refuted by the opinions of Pollexfen and all contemporary writers, (except those in the interest of the Company,) who unanimously declared that such exports, after 1666, amounted on the average to more than half a million pounds sterling a year.

When the East India Company gained a footing in the Orient, a monetary change was in progress which had commenced in the 14th century and was not yet completed. The Moslem conquests in the Orient had transported to the Mediterranean the accumulations of the precious metals in India and left that country under the necessity of employing currencies which consisted chiefly of copper coins and cowrie shells. In employing such measures of value no stable ratio of exchange could be established with Bassoura or Bagdad, a fact which greatly hampered the Arabian trade. To remedy this difficulty, and for other good reasons, Mahomet-bin-Tuglak, Emperor of Delhi, A. D. 1324-51, introduced in place of the copper coins a system of silver and silver-plated ones, which he hoped would displace the former. This was the first step towards a silver, or rather a billon coinage; and although not altogether successful, it led to better systems as time went on. In 1542 Sher Shah succeeded in establishing in the circulation the four-dirhem pieces, previously called tankahs and now first called rupees. In 1555-1604 Akbar the Great interdicted private coinage and made a notable but abortive attempt to establish all payments on the basis of silver coins struck by the State. In the reigns of his successors, Jehangeer, Shah Jehan and Auranzeb, this reform made but little progress, so that when, during the reign of this last named Emperor of Delhi, the East India Company began to strike coins at Bombay, the circulation generally, throughout the open parts of India, still largely consisted of copper and billon coins—the superior silver coins and the gold coins remaining in and about the capital cities and trading ports. To supply the deficiency of silver coins, by offering new and evenly-minted ones

" Macgregor's "Statistics," IV, 329.

for gold coins at a price (9 to 10 for 1), which seemed generous to the Indian shroffs, was an enterprise that profitably occupied the Company for nearly three-fourths of a century. Then (in 1749) having sold all its silver for gold, this virtuous Company plundered from the Indians all the silver it had sold them and once more reduced their oft plundered land to a currency of coppers and cowries. The present (silver) coinage dates substantially from 1766.

A fifth charter was granted to the East India Company August 9, 1683, and a sixth one April 12, 1686, which last one expired with the reign of William and Mary in 1693. " It was in the effort made by the Company to obtain a new charter from the government of William III., that the following occurrences took place. They are related in a pamphlet of 63 pages, entitled, "A Collection of the Debates and Proceedings in Parliament in the years 1694 and 1695, in relation to Corrupt Practices." "

It having transpired in the year 1694 that Sir John Trevor, the Speaker of the House of Commons, had accepted a bribe of a thousand guineas from the merchants belonging to the Corporation of London, to facilitate the enactment of the "Orphan's Bill," and there being rumors of bribery committed by the East India Company, the House, in order to purge itself of the reproach thus cast upon it, consigned Sir John to imprisonment in the Tower, and passed a resolution promising pardon and indemnity to anyone who should give evidence in relation to the bribery of members. The first result of this action was that Mr. Hungerford was convicted of having accepted a bribe of twenty guineas to pass the Orphan's Bill, whereupon he and Sir John Trevor were both expelled from the House. The next result was the commitment to the Tower of Sir Thomas Cooke, Governor of the East India Company in 1693, charged with having distributed bribes amounting, as subsequently proved, to some £200,000, to members of Parliament and other officers of the government. After much prevarication and delay, Cooke agreed to turn State's evidence, if a special bill of pardon and indemnity was enacted in his behalf. This being done in accordance with his wishes, he still paltered with the House, by confessing that he had spent £167,000 for "services rendered to the Company," chiefly towards its getting a new charter, but except in one instance, he could not say to whom the money was paid. The exception was with reference to £10,000 which was given (1693) to Mr. Francis

" Macgregor, IV, 332-3.
" Edition, London, 1698, qto. (Br. Mu. Press Mark, E, 1973).

Tysson, who told him he had given it to "Sir Josiah Child, who delivered it to the King" (William III.) "as a customary present, and
that *in King Charles' and other former reigns, the like had been done
for several years,* which by the books of the Company may appear."
This bribe was "presented to the king in tallies." Upon being further pressed, Sir Thomas Cooke furnished accounts of about £200,000
paid to what we would now call "the lobby," that is, to the relatives,
friends, agents or servants of "Parliament men"; for example, a
sum of £10,000 paid to Mr. Richard Acton, was for "Parliament
men"; and Sir Joseph Child had advised it. Among the high officials
and "Parliament men" implicated was Thomas Osborne, "Marquis
of Carmaerthen, now Lord Leeds." Enormous sums were paid to
Sir B. Firebrace for "Parliament men." When Firebrace was questioned, he implicated several noblemen and high officials, including
the Duke of Leeds, Lord President of the Privy Council, Sir Josiah
Child and Sir Thomas Cooke. The latter had also lodged a note in
Tysson's hands for £50,000, to be paid when the Act, which the
Company demanded, was passed. Money was also paid to Col.
Fitzpatrick, who had interest with Lady Derby, who had interest
with the Queen. The only result of these proceedings was that the
Duke of Leeds was impeached for accepting a bribe of 5,000 guineas,
to obtain a new charter and regulations for the East India Company.
The proceedings were then dropped.

It will hardly be contended that the corrupt state of the Parliament
thus disclosed, or the methods and means employed by the East
India Company, were new; for it is related of them so early as the
year 1657 that they had already carried their "increase of presents
to governors, *et cetera,* to an odious excess." [44] The case of Skinner
in 1660 is another evidence to the same effect. Here the espousal
by the Commons of the East India Company's interest, plainly
opposed to decency and justice, was the cause of a rupture between
the two Houses of Parliament, which lasted for several years and
almost put a stop to public business. [47] That the Parliament,
especially the Commons, was corrupt in the reign of Charles II., is
notorious; the fact is attested by numerous contemporary witnesses;
it is corroborated by the proceedings of Parliament itself and by the
remarks and criticisms of the few virtuous and patriotic Englishmen
who had the courage to lift their voices against the prevailing rottenness. The enormous powers and privileges granted by Charles II.

[44] Anderson, II, 443.   [47] Anderson, II, 461.

to the East India Company against the protests and representations
of persons well qualified to point out their mischievous and dangerous
influences, were evidently not granted for nothing; and even were
Sir Thomas Cooke's evidence wanting, it may fairly be concluded
that the exposure of the Company's methods, which took place in
1694, proved the means that were employed by them to procure the
Act of 1666-7, which really formed the basis of their prosperity, as
it constituted the most profitable of the various concessions granted
to them by the Crown, or the avid parasites who advised and
swayed it.

The reign of Charles II. was not only corrupt, it was corrupt to a
degree that affected all classes in proportion as they wielded power
or influence. In 1661 the king granted a new charter to the East
India Company, without consent of Parliament and contrary to law,
with leave to export £50,000 per annum of foreign silver, a privilege,
that subsequent events render it difficult to believe, was granted
without pecuniary consideration. In the same year he "shamefully
delivered up to France the country of Nova Scotia." [58] In 1662, he
sold to France for five million "livres," then more than twice as
heavy as modern "francs," say £400,000, "the town and port of
Dunkirk, with all its fortifications, sluices, dams, etc., and likewise
the fort of Mardyke with a wooden fort and the other great and
small forts between Dunkirk and Bergh St. Wynox, together with all
the arms, artillery, ammunition, etc." [59] In the same year he sold
the right of flooding Ireland with base coins to a company of London
goldsmiths, who probably turned their privilege to better account,
by floating their issues in the Oriental trade. [60] In 1664 the Duke
of York and probably also the king was pecuniarily interested in the
African Company, whose profits were chiefly derived from the slaves
captured in British Guinea and carried to British America. In 1665
the king granted a patent to "an ill-judged Canary Company," con-
ceding them the monopoly of trading to the Canary Islands for gold,
slaves and other commodities. "The third article of the House of
Commons' impeachment of the Lord Chancellor Clarendon, directly
charges him with having received great sums of money, for procuring
this and other illegal patents." [61] In the same year the king repudiated the "Bills of Public Faith" (greenbacks) issued by the Commonwealth and he granted to Prince Rupert the moneys recovered

[58] Anderson, II, 465.
[60] Ruding, II, 7.
[59] Anderson, II, 472.
[61] Anderson, II, 485.

from those who had purchased Crown lands with such bills of credit. "
In 1666, the same year that he signed the Coinage Act, and as contended, for the sake of a pension to Barbara Villiers, to come out of the
customs on liquors granted by the Commons and for other considerations, he also granted to another of his mistresses, Frances
Stewart, Duchess of Richmond, the sole coinage of tin farthings,
the effigy of " Britannia " on these coins being, as Evelyn intimates,
that of the frail but fair patentee. ". In 1667, when the Dutch
Admiral De Ruyter's bold exploits at Sheerness and Chatham caused
a general panic in London and a run upon the bankers who in
turn had deposited their funds in the Exchequer, the king "issued
his declaration for preserving inviolably the course of payments in
his Exchequer, both with regard to principal and interest "; yet de-
spite this solemn declaration he stopped payments from and closed
the Exchequer in 1672.   He then dishonestly appropriated " all the
funds entrusted to the public keeping." "

In 1668 he sold the " town, port and island of Bombay with the
rest of the isle of North Salsette," together with certain sovereign
rights, to the East India Company; and throughout his entire reign,
from the Restoration to the period of his death in 1684-5, he was
the recipient of an ignominious pension from Lous XIV. of France. "

Such are the circumstances under which this mischievous measure
of Free Coinage was generated, such was its character and such its
offspring: a bribe to the Crown; a premium on piracy; a stimulus to
the vile trade in mining-slaves; and the reward of intrigue and corruption, which were destined to breed, in turn, every form of injustice, rottenness and oppression.   It deprived the State of its ancient
control over money and has practically conferred this supernal
prerogative upon an aristocracy of wealth more detestable than the
tyranny from which our (American) forefathers rebelled.   It has
extorted from the people hundreds of millions for the expenses of
mint establishments in whose support they have no interest, or else
to make good the wear and tear of coins which are sold, like hogs,
by the pound weight and sent abroad to have their effigies of " Liberty " effaced and made to do service for the avowed enemies of
liberty.   Through the command of metallic money, which this
measure placed in the hands of the goldsmith or banking class, it
has enabled them to grasp the control of all money, of all substitutes

⁶¹ State papers, Dec. 1665.   ⁶² Humphrey, 472; Henfrey, 287.
⁶⁴ Anderson, II, 493, 519-20; Sinclair, I, 396.
⁶⁵ Anderson, II, 469; Sinclair, I, 313; Voltaire's Life of Louis XIV.

for money and of that commerce whose indispensable instrument is money. The remainder of the people are practically restricted to manual labor, the rétail trades, or other inferior or comparatively profitless employments.

What reason had the United States to copy this corrupt legislation in 1792 or to follow this mischievous policy? What business had *we* to copy England in the Coinage Act of 1666, whose main purpose and object was to evade and defeat the solemn decision of the Privy Council in the Mixt Money case? What had *we* to do with the profits of exchanging silver coins for Indian gold in the 17th century, or with the coining mill and screw press of Antoine Brucher, or with the West Indian piracies of Morgan and his fellow buccaneers, or with the slave trade of Guinea? What interest had *we* in the iniquities of the East India Company, its murders and robberies in the East, or its shameful purchase of a polluted king, a polluted cabinet and a polluted Parliament, in the West? What had *we* to do with the prostitution of Barbara Villiers, her greed, her avidity, her hold upon the British Mint, the monetary legislation that was framed to rid the king of her presence and instal another infamous woman in her infamous place? I say, what had *we Americans* to do with this burden of crimes and pollution which lay at the door of the Stuart family and belonged to a state of society from which we had revolted with abhorrence?

Nothing whatever. Yet we ignorantly adopted the whole of it on the day when Hamilton's mint bill was enacted by Congress. We copied it all; we made it our own; and in the course of the century which has passed since we adopted it, we have succeeded in building up a class of people who are interested, or who believe themselves to be interested, in supporting it. This class consists of merchants in the foreign trade and the bankers and others with whom they deal. Our foreign commerce does not consist, as does that of England, in the profitable functions of buying, selling and carrying for the rest of the world; but chiefly in buying for our own consumption classes of merchandise which could probably be better produced at home and in selling our grain and cotton and tobacco crops at half price. England has 320 millions of vassals laboring for her in India and Burmah, she has forty millions elsewhere, she has many millions of negroes in Africa who are virtually slaves, she has fifteen million tons of merchant shipping, a navy equal to that of any three other powers, and coaling-ports in every sea and clime. Unless we propose to reduce our own working class to the wages and condition of the

Indian ryot, the African slave, or the British pauper, we cannot compete with an industry that is built upon such a stupendous mass of iniquity, or which has attained such gigantic dimensions. And if both economical considerations and merciful feelings warn us to avoid a field in which there is neither honor nor profit for us, we should be prepared to renounce the British monetary system which is fitted alone for that field. Its basis is robbery of the weak and barter with the strong; its means are a monetary system entirely subjected to the bankers and foreign merchants of London; its aim is the elevation of this sordid and cynical class to the ownership and government of the earth. We Americans want no more of it! We demand that the government shall resume the control of money. We demand that silver shall be coined on precisely the same terms as gold, whatever those may be, and that both metals shall be subject to governmental seigniorage; we demand that the ratio of value in the coins of these metals shall be as it was before and is yet—16 for 1 of weight; we want no international treaties nor entanglements on the subject of money. In short, we demand that the Monetary Crimes of 1666, 1868, 1870 and 1873 shall be undone and the authors of the latter proclaimed and exposed to the execrations of an outraged people!

THE CRIME OF 1742.

THE early trade of the Colonies had been effected by barter, but by the last quarter of the 17th century the population had grown too numerous, widespread and differentiated in occupation to render such an archaic system of exchange any longer practicable.

So early as 1652 (October 19) the province of Massachusetts found it necessary—for it was no mere act of wantonness or of profit-seeking by the colony—to defy the Royal authority by erecting a Mint and striking Pine Tree shillings. These were to contain 66⅔ gr. fine silver, the same as the actual circulating clipped shilling of England, though not the same as the theoretical or minted shilling of the Commonwealth, which should have contained about 85¾ gr. fine.

From this moment began in America a contest between Barter and Exchange, between Capital and Blood, between the Plunder of the Seas and the Credit of the Colonies, between the Metallic product of slavery and the Fiduciary issues of a free people, that has not yet ended and that never will end until the principles which Aristotle distilled from the republics of antiquity have again asserted their vitality in the halls of legislation. These principles were revived in the Mixt Moneys case in 1604. They were affirmed by Bastiat in 1840: "Exchange is political economy; it is society itself, for it is impossible to conceive of society as existing without exchange, or exchange without society." They were again affirmed by Destutt Tracy in 1870: "Society is in fact held together by a series of exchanges." And they will be again and again affirmed until they are nailed inseparably to the Constitution of every free State in Christendom. "Exchange is a social act; money is a social mechanism; it is a public measure of value, the unit of which is not one coin, nor one note, but all the coins and notes of like currency under the law of each nation when added together; money to be equitable must be of stable volume; stability can only be secured by national authority and limitation; if you want prosperity you must trust the

national government to conserve the Measure of Value;. If you fear
to trust the government, you may indeed preserve the size of the
coin in your pocket, but you cannot secure the profits it may earn
for you; and persistence in this course will force ruin upon others
and probably upon yourself."

During the interval between the first issue of Pine Tree money
and the Revolution, these principles were brought home over and
over again to the Tory classes in America, but without avail. The
Tories affected entire disbelief in the Quantitative Theory of metallic
money, yet they always wanted the quantity of metallic money reduced; they derided paper money when it was issued by the Colony,
but vaunted it when issued by themselves. Because they could buy
the votes of certain individuals they mistrusted the body politic.
This was a grave mistake; for the body politic taken collectively is
a totally different entity from the individuals of which it may be
composed. It acts upon entirely different principles; and so does
Money.

The Pine Tree coins were at first of the denomination of 12, 6 and
3 pence, and in 1662 also of 2 pence. All except the 2 pence pieces
are dated 1652, although they were continued to be coined every
year until 1686, about which time paper money began to be thought
of. The shilling was ordered to contain 72 grains of standard silver,
(0.925 fine) or 66⅔ grains of fine silver. The extant coins in the
best preservation contain about 60⅔ grains fine; that is to say, about
three-fourths as much fine silver as the newly minted Royal shilling
of the same period; and at this valuation they were made legal
tender by colonial law and readily passed current. The seigniorage
on the Royal coins was 2 shillings in 60 shillings, or about 3⅓ per
cent.; on the Colonial coins it was 1 shilling in 20 shillings, or 5 per
cent. ad valorem; so that in fact the Crown manufactured coins at a
cheaper rate than did John Hull.

From the moment of the authorization of Hull's mint by the
Colonial Legislature, an event which dates from the period of the
Commonwealth in England, to that of its suppression, which was
achieved during the reign of William and Mary, an incessant warfare
was waged, now by the colonial Tories and then by the Royalists in
England, against American money. Its coinage defied the Royal
prerogative; it was the money of treason; it was coined from pirat-
ical plunder; it was dishonest money; it lowered the Royal standard;
it inflated the currency; Hull's charge for coinage was exhorbitant,
etc. Much of this was true; yet except the first one or two, these

charges were equally true of the British shilling of that day. That also was struck from plundered metal; it was therefore dishonest; it had been recently degraded; and was even clipped and sweated. Worse still were the tin coins struck for the American Colonies by James II., 1685-88, of which 192 were ordered to pass for a Spanish peso, or 24 to the real de plata. But in those days there was a great difference between my ox and yours.

The contest over the Pine Tree money was afterwards merged into a greater contest over the Colonial Bills of Credit which arose after and by reason of its suppression. This will receive some further notice when that later usurpation of the Royal prerogative comes to be mentioned.

The Colonial mint (or mints, for I fancy there was another, though a smaller one, in Maryland) was an open one; that is to say, it coined, or professed itself willing to coin, all bullion offered to it for that purpose. Such coins were declared to be legal tender by the Colonial assembly. As the mint did not coin gratuitously, it might be supposed that the seigniorage was enough to keep the coins from being melted or exported. But such was not the case; for although several hundred thousand, perhaps a million or more pounds sterling worth of Pine Tree money was struck from first to last by John Hull, it was all or nearly all exported; and very little of it remained at any time in circulation. One reason for this was that until 1666 the Royal mint also charged a seigniorage; and a second reason was that the West Indian buccaneers, who were the largest depositors at the Boston mint, wanted their remittances promptly returned to them in coins. The result was that the Pine Tree money flowed out of the country almost as soon as it was coined. Much of it was subsequently melted in the mints of Europe.

For these reasons so few coins of any kind remained in circulation during the Pine Tree money emissions that this period may more fitly be embraced in a longer one, 1632-92, during which the principal medium of exchange was obliged to be "country pay," that is to say, merchandise at prices fixed from time to time by Colonial laws.

To enter into details of this wretched system of barter would neither conform to our present limits of space, nor serve any other useful purpose than to corroborate by tedious evidence, the truth of the principles herein advanced by generality. Suffice it to say that the result of being obliged to employ "country pay" was to cramp the trade of the Colonies into the smallest limits and to render impossible any progress of the people beyond the phase of hard manual labor, variegated by neighborly "swaps." Commerce with distant persons or markets was impracticable; transportation was undeveloped; credit was unknown; the marts and the profits of American trade were transferred to London and there they remained.

This system is well illustrated in the private journal kept by Madame Knight, an educated lady, who traveled on horseback from Boston to New York in 1704. While in New Haven she wrote as follows:

"They give the title of 'merchant' to every trader, who rates his goods according to the time and species they pay in; viz., 'pay'; 'money'; 'pay-as-money'; and 'trusting.' Pay is grain, pork and beef, etc., at the prices set by the General Court. Money is pieces-of-eight, ryals, Boston or Bay shillings, or 'good hard money,' as sometimes silver coin is called; also wampum, viz., Indian beads, which serve as change. Pay-as-money is provision aforesaid, one-third cheaper than the Assembly set it; and Trust, as they agree for at the time. When the buyer comes to ask for a commodity, sometimes before the merchant answers that he has it, he says, 'is your pay ready?' Perhaps the chap replies, 'yes.' 'What do you pay in?' says the merchant. The buyer having answered, then the price is set; as suppose he wants a 6d. knife, in ' pay ' it is 12d.; in ' pay-as-money' 8d., and 'hard-money,' its own value, 6d. It seems a very intricate way of trade, and what the Lex Mercatoria had not thought of."

But beneath this enforced archaism there were ideas; and in the inventive minds of the Americans these soon took form. The leather moneys of mediæval Europe were probably unknown to the Colonists; even the paper issues of Milan and Genoa may have been unheard of, or but dimly understood; but such could hardly have been the case with the leather and paper moneys of San Domingo issued about the year 1638, the Swedish "Transport Notes" of 1658, or the notes issued by Cromwell at about the same time. At all events a Land Bank was organized in South Carolina which issued "convertible" notes upon the security of estates, somewhere about the year 1675. The example was eagerly followed in Boston, where in 1686 John Blackwell and six other persons, one or more of whom were from London, established a Land Bank and issued their private notes "payable" in coins and "secured" by land. Either the "security" of these notes proved to be inadequate or doubtful, or else some other circumstance affected their credit; the fact is that the notes failed to become acceptable to the public and soon ceased to circulate as money. Whether they were paid off or repudiated does not appear.

Soon after this abortive attempt to introduce private promissory notes intó the circulation, the Colony of Massachusetts resolved to relieve "the scarcity of money and the want of an adequate measure of commerce" by issuing its own Bills of Credit to the modest extent of £7,000. This was done in February, 1690, the notes bearing the following legend:

"No. (916) - - - - - - 20s.

This indented Bill of Twenty Shillings due from the Massachusetts Colony to the Possessor shall be in value equal to money, and shall be accordingly accepted by the Treasurer and Receivers subordinate to him, in all payments and for any stock at any time in the Treasury, Boston, in New England, February the third, 1690. By order of the General Court.

[L. s.]   ELISHA HUTCHINSON, }
           JOHN WALLEY,   } Comitee."
           TIM THORNTON,   }

It was afterwards repeatedly alleged that this was a "war issue" to pay off the soldiers in the Phips expedition to Quebec, and therefore it was but just and proper to retire it as soon as practicable. Without entering into this sort of reasoning, because it is a non sequitur, the fact is that the issue of notes was made not only before the Phips soldiers demanded to be paid, but before the expedition sailed and indeed before it was planned. The notes were issued early in February, 1690; the expedition to Quebec was not resolved upon until May 1st; it sailed August 9th, landed and was defeated October 8th, re-embarked October 11th and arrived in New England November 19th. The soldiers' demand for pay was fully a year later than the date when the Bills of Credit were authorized to be issued.

In 1691 a further issue was made of Colonial Bills of Credit and in these notes some of the defeated heroes of Quebec were doubtless paid off, a circumstance which, however, has nothing to do with the question of their origin or justification.

It will be observed that the Bills were not money; but merely promises to pay money; in other words, they were not legal tender; nobody was obliged to accept them outside the Colonial Treasury. All this was changed after the new Charter of 1692 became effective. The provincial government then, July 2, 1692, made the notes, now amounting to £30,000 or £40,000 full legal tenders, except in special contracts. Under these circumstances they circulated at par with silver coins (the parity being 8 shillings per "ounce" of standard silver coins) until 1712, a period of twenty years, during which time the population of the Colony more than doubled and the trade increased enormously.

By the year 1712 a large increase in the issue of these notes and the admission of other elements into the currency, both foreign and Colonial, metallic and paper, occasioned the depreciation of the notes and clipping of the coins to the extent of about one-eighth. Counterfeit notes of Massachusetts, New Hampshire, Connecticut and Rhode Island also swelled the total.

In 1714 the Colony of Massachusetts made a new and further issue of provincial notes commencing with £50,000 which was soon increased to £125,000. A private bank of issue based upon landed assets was also authorized between 1714 and 1720. In 1692 the population was about 47,000, the note circulation £30,000, and silver coin 6 shillings 10½d. in paper notes per "ounce." In 1728 the population was about 115,000, the note circulation £400,000, and silver coin 16 shillings per ounce. These excessive issues and the bursting of the Mississippi Bubble in France now led the government of England to interfere. It commenced in 1727 that series of repressive measures which furnished the first distinctive provocation to the American Revolution.

These measures were not undertaken so much with the view of reforming the currency of the Colonies as of enforcing the prerogative of the king, which would have been right enough in England but wholly indefensible when applied to a distant colony. However, this object was sought to be accomplished by means alike offensive and oppressive. The Colonial governors were ordered to sign no more laws authorizing Bills of Credit; the outstanding Bills of Credit were ordered to be withdrawn; the taxes were ordered to be paid in coins; in short, without a single extenuating reason, the British ministry followed in America precisely the same steps that after the downfall of John Law were pursued with such fatal results by Louis XV. of France. When in 1727 Gov. Dummer refused to sign an authorization for £50,000 of new bills to help pay off £100,000 of old bills, the House of Assembly declared that THEY CONSIDERED THEIR LIBERTIES THREATENED. The Governor's reply to this note of alarm was to force the House in 1728 to further contract the currency.

In 1730, Gov. Belcher was appointed by the Crown with imperative orders to go on with the contraction until the note currency was

reduced to £30,000. The Colonial Assembly again and again petitioned the Crown to revoke this ruinous order, but without avail.
The method of contraction rendered it still more objectionable. The
notes were not retired by paying for them with a surplus of coin in
the Treasury, for there was no such surplus. They were to be paid
off from the proceeds of new and additional taxation. On top of all
this was another grievance; the void in the circulation was to be
partly filled by the notes of private banks, which were authorized to
be established upon a "silver basis " by the favorites or dependents
of the English governor, such notes having no legal tender quality.
In 1737 the provincial notes had been reduced to not much over the
£30,000 limit, and the private bank issues were about £110,000;
while the other elements of the currency hardly brought the whole
to much more than half of what it had been before contraction began.
In 1735, the worst period of contraction, money was so scarce that
the inhabitants could not, even when threatened with a forced sale
of their goods, pay their taxes, except in commodities; and the governor reluctantly accepting the situation, agreed to receive the taxes
in hemp, flax and bar-iron.   It reminds one of the ox-hides exacted
by the Roman governor from the Frisians sixteen hundred years
previously.* The discretion with which such a system necessarily
armed the collecting officials must have afforded the latter opportu-
nities for exercising the most galling oppression.

We have no space for entering upon the intricacies of Old, Middle
and New Tenor bills, nor for considering the influence of the Merchants' Bank notes, nor of the municipal notes of this æra† upon
the circulation; it is far more important to trace the Equity or Demonetization Act that, in 1742 Gov. Shirley tricked the Colonial Assembly into passing.

This Act contained a clause which read: "If they (the Colonial
Bills of Credit) depreciate, allowance shall be made accordingly," a
clause whose significance seems to have escaped the attention of the
Assembly.   Its practical effect was to demonetize the Colonial bills
and make all contracts payable in standard silver coins at 6s. 8d. per
ounce, or in so much paper money as would purchase this quantity
of silver coins at the time that payment was made.   Nothing could
have been more iniquitous.

---

* See " History Monetary Systems," ch. V.

† I have seen a circulating note dated Ipswich, Massachusetts, May 1, 1741, for
some small amount, in possession of my friend Mr. L. L. Robinson, of San Francisco.

Shirley's next move was to induce the new "Land Bank" to retire
its issues, amounting to £40,000. Similar pressure caused the
"Silver" banks to retire their notes, amounting to £120,000. As
this process went on, the grip upon the people gradually tightened;
and from this they sought relief by according "free course," or currency, to the Provincial Bills of the contiguous Colonies. But here
again they were defeated by the governor's untiring zeal and energy
in the cause of contraction. Under the threat of losing their Charter, he induced them, partly in 1744 and partly in 1746, to relinquish
this last resource. The results that followed were most distressing.
Prices fell, trade became stagnant, securities depreciated and loans
were recalled; debtors were sold out by the sheriff; "many good
families were brought to poverty"; and cries of distress arose on all
sides. The governor was petitioned to repeal the misnamed "Equity
Bill," but he refused; the representatives appealed to Parliament,
but met with no relief. The fiat had gone forth; the king's prerogative of the coinage, though surrendered in England to the East India
Company was to be maintained in the Colonies; the latter were to
have no monetary system of their own; and, under the operation of
the British Act of 1666, the goldsmiths of London and their newly
fledged and already embarrassed Bank of England, were to rule the
situation.*

What is expansion? It is forcing into circulation an unusually
large volume of money, or else exposing it to be so inflated. What
is contraction? It is reducing the volume of money, or exposing it
to be reduced below the customary amount in circulation. The
swollen measure of value is quite as unjust as the shrunken measure.
There is no necessity for either; but so long as a nation neglects to
regulate by law the volume of its currency, its people will always
live in danger of one or the other of these inequitable measures of
value, the swollen one or the shrunken one. After such an unjusti-
fiable expansion as had been caused by the provincial bills of credit,
it did not appear to be at all inequitable to pay off the bills in coins
and return to coin payments; for everybody assumed that the coins
would remain in the Colony and supply the place of the bills. But
such was not the case. The Colony was in debt both to the subjects
and the government of the mother country; and as fast as the coins
entered the circulation as a measure of value in Massachusetts, they
were shipped to London as a commodity to meet the bills of exchange

* The Bank of England has failed several times, the first failure having occurred
in 1696.

drawn by the depositors of the bullion and eventually to feed the open mint in the Tower. The Resumption Act, approved by the king, June 28, 1749, was therefore not a mere contraction; it was a terrible calamity.

The Act was followed by a sop to Cerberus, in the shape of a shipment from London of 653,000 ounces of silver and 10 tons of copper coins, due to the Colonial government, for the expenses of the Phips expedition. The Colonial government nevertheless was ordered to pay these coins out only to redeem its own Bills of Credit and at a discount prices, and to demand payment in coins for taxes and dues at par. This operation was commenced in 1750. By itself it would seem both fair and harmless, but in connection with Shirley's surreptitious demonetization of the Colonial bills, previously mentioned, it converted all debts created at inflation prices into obligations payable during the prevalence of contraction prices, a contraction enormously aggravated by the constant tendency of the coins to flow out of the Colony to the mother country. The result was a complete revulsion of fortune among every class of Americans. The favored official or lucky adventurer became rich, the industrious trader was impoverished, the creditor was lifted up, the debtor was cast down; and every sort of injustice was committed under cover of law. Worse than all, while the inflation had been gradual, and covered a period of many years, the contraction was made both sudden and severe.

The Land and Silver bank notes were already retired; the provincial notes of the other American Colonies were decried; and £440,000 of Massachusetts bills, which though demonetized in 1742 were still in circulation, were bought up and retired with about £40,000 in coins. The effect was frightful. Ruin stalked in every home, the people could not pay their taxes; and were obliged to see their property seized by the sheriff and sold at one-tenth its previous value. Commerce was annihilated; and in its place was substituted a petty barter that was maintained with "country pay." Even the taxes were obliged to be collected in kind. In the face of this great distress the governor relented so far as to permit £3,000 in small notes to be issued for change; but from the beginning to the end of his administration he never faltered a moment in the execution of the orders he had received; and these were to destroy the fiduciary issues of the Colonies without regard to consequences. The Colonists were to create wealth; it was reserved for Englishmen to exchange and enhance it.

Driven into a corner and deprived of all hope of such a stay of prices as would enable them to effect their exchanges and pay their debts without sacrificing their entire fortunes, the people replied to these measures with subterfuge, violence and defiance of the law. In 1755 large quantities of base coins were imported from France; in 1760 counterfeit "cobs," or dollars, were fabricated at Scarborough; in 1761 the Assembly admitted that counterfeiting had become rife; and in 1762 it was deemed necessary to pass an Act with almost capital penalties against the commission of this offense. In 1751 a Riot Act was passed to suppress the outbreaks occasioned by the Resumption Act; tumultuous assemblies occurred in and near Boston; and the people of Abingdon broke into open revolt.

At this point the Royal government made a concession. To have refused to make it, would have precipitated the Revolution at once; for the people had been pushed to the last point of forbearance. Says a writer on the currency: " Their prosperity had been checked, their trade destroyed, their property sold under the hammer, many of them had been driven away and the remainder were oppressed with a load of taxes which were payable in unattainable coins. They were ripe for revolt. The concession now made to them merely postponed the Revolution; it did not remove its causes."

On April 24, 1751, a bill had passed the Assembly authorizing the Treasurer to liquidate the current expenses of the Colony by the issue of interest-bearing certificates of indebtedness in denominations of £6 (afterwards £4) payable in one year. To this bill the governor had yielded a reluctant consent. Its operation afforded immediate relief to the affairs of the Colony, for to the surprise of the governor and possibly also to that of the Assembly, these certificates circulated freely among the people as money. So soon as this practice became known in London it was attempted to be stopped. In June, 1751, the Parliament of England forbade the circulation of the Colonial debt certificates as money; and to leave no excuse for thus employing them, measures were taken to encourage loans of metallic money to the Colony of Massachusetts upon long bonds, which were to be liquidated out of the proceeds of future Colonial revenues. But loans of money with a string tied to each coin was not what the Americans desired. They had had enough of that sort of relief. Their Treasurer's certificates were quite good enough for them; and in spite of Parliament, these circulated as money so freely that by the year 1766 not less than £157,000 in this "illegitimate" currency was afloat. Mr. Felt hints at a much higher figure, but I can see no reason to follow him.   The emission of these notes eventually led to such an improvement of affairs that in 1774 Gov. Hutchinson remarked in his message: "There never has been a time since the first settlement of the country when the Treasury has been in so good a state as it now is."   But the Colony had not forgotten the sufferings it had endured through the monetary policy which this very man had done so much to enforce; and at the moment that he wrote this complacent sentence it was preparing to throw off forever the shackles which had been imposed upon it by British policy and British legislation.   All that was needed was a plausible pretext, and that it found in the Stamp Act.*

* From Del Mar's "History of Money in America."

THE CRIME OF 1868.

PREVIOUS to the Presidential campaign of 1868 the following facts relative to the position of the *New York World* were very generally known or believed.

I. That Mr. Manton Marble was not the sole or even the principle owner of the paper. This is established among other evidence by his own averment in the suit of George Opdyke *vs.* The *World.*

II. Among those known or believed to own shares in the paper were August Belmont Senior and S. L. M. Barlow. Samuel J. Tilden was also regarded as possessing some proprietary interest in it. Mr. Belmont was looked upon as the principal owner. Between Mr. Belmont and Mr. Marble the strongest ties of interest and friendship were known to exist. Mr. Belmont was understood to be the purse and Mr. Marble the brains of the newspaper.

III. Mr. Belmont was and had been for many years the agent for an European banking Syndicate. This Syndicate was the owner of a large amount in American War bonds and had acted as the agent and banker of numerous other European houses interested in the same bonds. These bonds by the terms of their issue (Act of Feb. 25, 1862), were payable in greenbacks; and, although this view of the law on the subject was disputed in after years by the holders of the bonds or their advocates, it was from the legal point of view probably the correct one. This view is supported by the speeches of Senators Collamer, Wilson and others during the passage of the Act through the Senate (See *Congressional Globe* 1861-2); by the speeches of Messrs. Spaulding, Stevens, Pendleton and others in the House when the bill was before that body; and by the fact that the bonds when issued were subscribed and paid for in greenbacks, and thus fetched but half-price in gold coin, while at the same time other American bonds, payable specifically in gold, or about the terms of the payment of which there was no dispute, commanded full price. Among these were the 5 per cent bonds of the State of Massachusetts.

Whatever was the precise legal bearing of the terms in which the Five-Twenties were made payable it was evidently of the highest importance to those who had purchased them at half-price to procure them if possible to be made payable at full price. This was only to be done by an Act of Congress which should explicitly make the bonds payable in coin and remove all doubt about the terms of payment. On the other hand, it was, by the same token, against the interest of the people of the United States to make any alteration in the law covering the bonds. If there was any doubt about the terms of liquidation, the country would only increase its burden of payment by removing it; if there was no doubt, no legislation was needed.

The nominal sum of the Five-Twenty bonds which were in dispute and had been sold at half-price on account both of the terms of emission and of the doubt as to their terms of payment, was, as the writer is now informed, about $550,000,000. The government had received but about $275,000,000 in gold for them; and the profit (besides the double interest, semi-annually in gold coin, all along), which the holders might very certainly count upon realizing, in case they could obtain the legislation they desired, amounted to $275,-000,000 more. It will be admitted that this was a stake worth intriguing for; perhaps the greatest reward which ever tempted men to conspire and betray.

Down to the winter of 1867-8 Mr. Belmont had exhibited very little interest in the bond question, or, indeed, any other question that then interested the Conservative party. He had been appointed Chairman of its National Committee at a time when the fortunes and prospects of the party were very low and chiefly on account of the liberality with which he contributed to its beggared finances. Down to the election of 1868 he is believed to have contributed about $25,000, of which $10,000 were in one sum. But neither by his own utterances nor through those of the newspapers, which it was believed he in great measure owned and controlled, did Mr. Belmont manifest any active interest in politics. It was quite evident that he regarded the Conservative party, as for the present, quite dead; and that he had sought its leadership less for any practical results which it might then promote, than for what such leadership might be worth to him, or the Syndicate he represented, in the future.

This future came in the Fall of 1867. Down to that period the New York *World*, through Mr. Marble, had been specifically pledged

to support Mr. Pendleton for the Presidency. (See letter of
"Buckeye" in Cincinnati *Enquirer* of about August 20, 1874.) All
of a sudden its course was changed with reference to Pendletonism,
the bond question, legal-tenders and everything else connected with
the subject.

Mr. Marble explains his sudden conversion from Pendletonism and
the greenback theory by the fact that he met a Man on a mountain
in New Hampshire; (See New York *World* August 24, 1874;) but
those who know the circumstances best believe that the Man was in
Paris and operated through an agent in Wall Street, New York.

Shortly after this and acting probably in pursuance of instructions
from the Man in Paris Mr. Belmont went to Washington, where he
entertained at a banquet the Members of the Democratic Congressional Committee and other leading Democrats in and out of Congress; and availed himself of the occasion to persuade them to
change the place of holding the National Convention from some
Southern or Western city, which they had previously expressed a
decided preference for, to New York.

The first steps in the Conspiracy were taken none too soon. The
Conservative party, which had previously been drifting about in
search of an anchorage not too near the dangerous and wreck-
bestrewn coast of Africa, had come upon the promising island of
Greenbacks and after much careful reconnoitering determined to
land there and intrench itself. This situation became so popular
that vast numbers of the people adopted it, until at length and for
the first time in many years it seemed possible for the Conservative
party to succeed in a general contest with its great Republican adver-
sary. To induce the Conservatives to abandon this position before
it grew too strong and to persuade it to choose a battle-ground on
other territory, was obviously the first move of the Conspirators.
From this time forth the *World* became a "hard money" paper.

On the 13th of March, 1868, Baron James Rothschild of Paris
wrote to Mr. Belmont a letter which was exhibited by the latter to
several gentlemen in New York. This letter had evidently been
prepared for the purpose of being shown to leading members of the
party, in order to influence their opinion on the bond question. It
contained a long argument against the then pending proposition to
make the Five-Twenties refundable for 50-year 4 per cent bonds
without changing the original terms of payment, declared this a
compulsory measure tinctured with "repudiation" and concluded
with warnings of ruin to those who might oppose the payment of

the bonds in coin, or who might advocate their liquidation in green-backs.

On July 4, 1868, the Democratic National Convention met at Tammany Hall, New York, with Mr. Belmont as chairman. On the 7th of July and to the complete chagrin of the conspirators it passed the following resolution: "Where the obligations of the Government do not expressly state upon their face, or the law under which they were issued does not provide that they shall be paid in coin, they ought in right and in justice, be paid in the lawful money of the United States."

It will be seen from this resolution that, notwithstanding the efforts of Belmont and Marble during the Winter of 1867-8 and the follow-ing spring, to influence the opinion of the Conservative party on this subject, it had deliberately followed its own course, heedless of these intriguants. Further than this it showed an evident determination to nominate a candidate for the Presidency who was especially the exponent of the views expressed in the above plank of the party platform. This was George H. Pendleton. He was nominated on the first ballot, receiving 105 votes, which were increased to 156½ (211½ or ⅔ of 317 being necessary to a choice), a number not ex-ceeded by any candidate, until, on the 22nd ballot and with Pendle-ton's own previously written permission to warrant the act, Gen. McCook of Ohio suddenly withdrew Pendleton's name, in its place nominated that of Horatio Seymour, an advocate of coin payments and elected the latter as the Candidate of the Convention on a single ballot.

It was rumored at the time that the use by McCook of Pendleton's generous "permission" in the form of a "request" and the unex-pected nomination of Seymour, were the fruits of the intrigue of which Belmont and Marble were even then suspected. But the writer's purpose is not to repeat rumors. He intends to confine himself to what he *knows* about the betrayal of the Conservative party in 1868; and what he knows relates not to the Convention nor to its proceedings, but to what occurred before the Convention met and after it adjourned.

This last mentioned event occurred on the 9th of July. On the 4th of August Mr. Seymour's letter of acceptance appeared and the campaign began. It has been stated that Mr. Seymour was an ad-vocate of coin payments. So he was. In accepting him for its can-didate the leaders had indeed changed the party flag, but the maskers had not left their Island; nor were they inclined to do so. It soon became evident that, Pendleton or no Pendleton, the Conservative party were determined to stand by greenbacks; and the most popular badge of the campaign was an imitation greenback dollar-note with the portrait of Seymour on its face and the legend "This note is a legal tender," etc. on the back. It is true that in the event of a Conservative victory the conspirators had counted upon Mr. Seymour to approve of a bill providing coin payments for the Five-Twenty bonds and greenbacks; but the position of the Convention was that but few Conservative members of Congress would be likely to vote for such a measure so long as the constituencies were manifestly opposed to it. In short the conspirators were baffled

There was but one way for them out of this dilemma and that way was to treacherously destroy Mr. Seymour's chance of being elected, by suddenly creating a panic on the eve of the contest.

The successive steps of the conspiracy now began to appear. 1st. The sudden abandonment by the *World* of the support of Mr. Pendleton and Pendletonism. 2nd. Its attempts to persuade the party to commit itself to the policy of coin payments. 3rd. Mr. Belmont's cajolement of the Washington leaders into changing the seat of the National Convention to New York, in order to bring its members and proceedings under the more immediate influence of himself, the *World* and the other instrumentalities of the conspiracy. 4th. The snap election in the Convention of its presiding officer and against his own wishes. 5th. The delegation by the National Convention of its entire power and authority and that of the Executive Committee, the State Committee and the Auxiliary Committee, acting directly or indirectly under it, into the single hand of Mr. Belmont, the agent of a colossal banking Syndicate, with ample experience in court and state intrigues. 6th. The foisting of the *World*, one of Mr. Belmont's instrumentalities, upon the party, as the acknowledged and accepted organ and exponent of its policy and views; and 7th, The use of the *World* for the purpose of suddenly and on the eve of Election (and when it was too late to put up other candidates) betraying and abandoning the ticket, throwing the party into confusion and converting a victory into defeat. Four of these steps have been already described. The writer now proceeds to relate the history of the remaining three.

The withdrawal of Pendleton, who was a candidate of enthusiasm, and the substitution of Seymour, who, distrusting his nominators, had evinced but little warmth in the contest, had weakened the prospects of the ticket; but the unexpected impeachment of the Radi-

cals, made in my official Finance Letter of September, 1868, had so
improved these prospects that in the early part of October the election was generally conceded to the Conservatives. The Radical
party had been successfully arraigned as violators of the Constitution, corrupt, extravagant and responsible for a condition of the
finances which had demoralized the public and exposed the country
to the gravest dangers. The fortunes of the Radical party had
never appeared so low as at this juncture; and already sugges-
tions were being made for the cabinet which President Seymour
would soon find it necessary to call to his aid in the administration
of the Federal Government.

In the midst of this promise of success to the Conservatives and
appearance of defeat to the Radicals, quite unexpectedly, without
previous warning or intimation of any kind, and like a bolt shot from
a summer sky, the New York *World* of Thursday, October 15, 1868,
published a brief but portentous editorial article, in which, falsely
and basely premising that success could not possibly await the Conservative party with Horatio Seymour at its head, it treacherously
and perfidiously advised that the name of this honored statesman
should be withdrawn and some other substituted in its place for
President of the United States.

Remember that the *World* had claimed to be and had been fully
trusted as the organ and mouthpiece of the party; that it was believed to be owned and controlled by men presumed to be interested
in the success of the party; that the prospects of the party had not
for many years seemed so brilliant; that not a word from any quarter had been intimated against Mr. Seymour; that the Convention
had been dissolved for over three months; that it could not be re-
organized in less than one or two months; that no provision had been
made to organize it again that year; that without it, no one had
authority to change the Presidential Candidate or withdraw his name
from the ticket; and that it was now within a fortnight of Election
day.

The treason of Dumouriez, who plotted with the enemy to overthrow the French Republic, which had placed him in supreme command of its armies; the treason of Burr "who permitted himself to
be used by his political opponents in order to defeat the candidate
of his own party whom he himself had supported" and who then
attempted the subversion of his country through a secret alliance
with Mexico—these treasonable attempts were petty in comparison
with that of Marble. Dumouriez and Burr were both suspected men

and the confidence reposed in them was by no means unlimited; in regard to Marble there was no suspicion whatever. Dumouriez was fired upon by his own soldiers; Burr exposed himself to capital punishment in a trial for high treason. Marble ran the risk of no penalty save the execrations of his betrayed countrymen. The law protects his life as it does that of any other man and his skin is as safe today as its triple covering of brass can render it. Dumouriez and Burr betrayed their countries for the sake of ambitions which could be gratified with nothing less than absolute and ungoverned control; a passion which has at least the merit of greatness about it. Marble's motive for betraying the party will appear as we proceed. Dumouriez and Burr both failed in their treachery; Marble not only succeeded, but has since had the unparalleled audacity to demand and accept a position of trust from the party that he betrayed.

Nothing could exceed the consternation produced by the *World* article of October 15, 1868. It was as though the general of a division had gone over to the enemy on the eve of an assured victory. The article was telegraphed all over the country on the morning of its appearance and by noon of the same day it was believed, in all the principal cities and towns throughout the country, that the Conservative party had been betrayed and abandoned by its chosen leaders, Belmont, Tilden, Schell and Marble: for no one supposed for a moment that Marble would have dared to publish such an article without authority from the chief representatives of the party in New York.

Such at least was the impression produced in Washington, where the writer resided at the time; and the Washington leaders of the Conservative party were experienced men and not likely to draw an erroneous inference from any writing in plain English.

The famous article was received in Washington at about 10 o'clock on the morning of its publication in New York. It was seen at noon by Mr. Jonah D. Hoover, chairman of the Congressional Committee and publisher of the *Express*, an afternoon Conservative newspaper. Mr. Hoover was astounded with the appearance of the article and hesitated about republishing it in the *Express*. The graver question, though, was with regard to the Committee of which he was chairman. What action should the Committee take in the matter? Should it ignore or repudiate the newspaper article and endeavor to rally the party around the ticket? Yet if the article was the deliberate act of the party leaders in New York, this course might prove to be the merest folly, and what chance had any such provincial rally against a desertion so open and public, done at the radiating point of a thousand printing-presses and telegraph wires, done at the seat of the party convention, at the residence of the chairman of the Convention, in the State whence the Presidential Candidate had been chosen, and by the trusted newspaper organ of the party and mouthpiece of the party owned wholly or for the most part by its leaders?

Mr. Hoover decided upon calling a meeting of the Congressional Committee and party chiefs that night at the office of the *National Intelligencer*, the principal conservative newspaper of the District; and the writer hereof was one of those who were invited to attend.

Meanwhile Mr. Hoover telegraphed to Mr. Belmont at New York demanding to know the meaning of the *World* article, and whether the National Committee was responsible for it.

It is necessary to explain here that the Democratic Convention, when it adjourned, adjourned *sine die*, and left in charge of its affairs a National Committee composed of one member from each state of the Union. Of this National Committee, whose headquarters were in New York, Mr. Belmont was Chairman. This National Commitee appointed an Executive Committtee of ten members, with Mr. Belmont as Chairman and a Washington Congressional Committee of eleven members (who afterward added three adherents to their number) with Mr. Hoover as Chairman. There was also in New York a State Committee, of which Belmont, Tilden, Schell and others were members and an Auxiliary Committee composed of Belmont, Tilden, Schell and others who were members of one or more of the other committees, and still others who were not. Thus the business of the Convention was entrusted to the National Committee; that of the National Committee to the Executive Committee; that of the Executive Committee to the Auxiliary Committee, and that of the Auxiliary Committee to Belmont, who left the formal and clerical portion of it to Tilden and Schell, and kept the vital and important portion of it to himself.

Tilden and Schell opened an office for the distribution of documents and like business, at the corner of Fourth Avenue and Seventeenth Street. Belmont went to New York, where he remained all summer, with the National Convention and all its Committees in his breeches pocket; and there sat down with his friend and faithful follower Marble to exchange cable telegrams with the Man in Paris and plot the betrayal and defeat of the Conservative party.

The meeting at the *Intelligencer* office was appointed for 9 P. M. of the same day on which the *World* article was published. Down to the hour of meeting no reply had been received to Mr. Hoover's telegram.   There were present at the meeting Hon. Alex. W. Randall, Postmaster General; Hon. Richard T. Merrick; Hon. Alex. Del Mar, Director of Statistics; John F. Coyle, Esq., one of the proprietors of the *Intelligencer*, and his partner Mr. Snow; Mr. W. W. Warden, one of President Johnson's private secretaries, Colonel Whitely, Marshall Hoover and several others.

Marshall Hoover stated the object of the meeting.   The *World* article, evidently inspired by the leaders of the party at New York, had virtually deprived the party of its Chieftain on the very eve of election and the moment of success.   He had telegraphed to Belmont and Tilden, but had received no answer.   The abandonment of the ticket was being telegraphed all over the country and every moment was precious.   What was to be done?   Accept the situation and endeavor to keep the party together by at once nominating another candidate on their own responsibility, relying upon the urgency of the occasion and the influence of the *Intelligencer* and the Southern press (which would probably endorse its action), to ratify their nomination; or, wait another twenty-four hours, until demoralization and defection had spread far and wide, and unity of action was no longer possible?   Knowing that in such an emergency every hour was precious, he said that Messrs. Belmont and Tilden's delay in responding to his telegram was in the highest degree censurable.

Another gentleman said that he took it for granted that nobody present doubted that the *World* article was authorized.   (No sign of dissent from anybody present.)   If it was authorized, there was no use in telegraphing to Belmont about it or in awaiting an answer from him.   It was quite plain that the party leaders in New York had determined to abandon the ticket; though what their motive was, consistent with any regard for their honor or probity, or what they expected to effect by it, exceeded his comprehension.   He feared that there was foul work beneath it.   But the country must not be allowed to suffer from this great act of treachery.   The blow that had been struck was a base, but not a fatal one.   Seymour was now out of the field, but he thought that with prompt action the party might be induced to unite upon another candidate; and as every hour's delay urged it further upon the rocks of anarchy and ruin, he had consulted Chief Justice Chase with the view of obtaining his consent to run.   Judge Chase had replied that it was too late; that such a movement was impracticable and useless; that no one had authority to act; that the National Convention must be called together again. The speaker had, however, inferred from Judge Chase's remarks that in case the party made an authoritative demand for it, the Chief Justice would allow his own name to be used on the ticket, provided Mr. Seymour and all parties assented. In the hope that this measure could be effected the speaker had prepared an article for insertion in the *Intelligencer*, proof-slips of which he then handed around.

The writer has one of these slips now. It rehearses the *World* article, accepts the situation, and nominates Chase for President, with Hancock, Adams, Hendricks, Ewing or Franklin for Vice President.

Another gentleman then got up and remarked that although there could be little doubt that the *World* article was authorized by the party leaders in New York; although the crisis was momentous and every hour of delay fraught with new danger; yet they could not be sure that the *World* article was authorized. They had better wait until next day before putting forward Judge Chase's name. The suggestion as to the omission of Judge Chase's name prevailed.

Another speaker contended that the *Intelligencer* could not ignore the subject. In deserting Mr. Seymour the *World* had abandoned the political principles which Mr. Seymour represented. If the *Intelligencer* accepted the situation it would also desert those principles; and unless it substituted other principles in their stead, the party would be left without a rallying cry; and not only would the party fail in the election, it would disintegrate and break up entirely.

This suggestion also prevailed and the proposed article was modified, not only by omitting Judge Chase's name, it exhorted the party to rally around the Constitution of 1789, and insisted upon the preservation of the Union under its organic law: mere generalities. Proof-slips of the article, as revised, were then handed to Mr. Warden for the Associated Press and in a quarter of an hour's time it had flown to the four quarters of the Continent.

The meeting broke up at 11 o'clock, and everybody felt that the campaign was over and lost. Too much power had been delegated to Belmont and he had shamefully and fatally abused it.

After midnight Marshall Hoover received the following dispatch from Mr. Samuel J. Tilden.

NEW YORK, October 16, 1868.

JONAH D. HOOVER, Esq., Washington, D. C.

No authority or possibility to change front.   All friends consider it totally impracticable and equivalent to disbanding our forces.   We in New York are not panic-stricken.

> S. J. TILDEN,
> AUGUST BELMONT,
> AUGUSTUS SCHELL.

This dispatch was put upon the wires in New York nearly twenty-four hours after the *World* article appeared; whereas, if the *World* article was unauthorized, it should have been given to the country instantly upon the appearance of the article.   The dispatch merely said that a change of front was impracticable and omitted to state with sufficient explicitness whether any consultation had been held with the *World* in reference to the publication of its treasonable editorial.   It was therefore still more uncertain whether the *World* article emanated from the Committee or not.   At all events the telegram was received in Washington too late to change the course of the *Intelligencer.*   The article which the Congressional Committee had concluded to print had already flown all over the country and it therefore had to be printed in the morning issue of the paper.

On the next day (Friday) one of the Washington conclave was requested by the Committee and also by President Johnson to call upon the members of the Auxiliary Committee at New York and clear up all doubts as to the real position of affairs.

At this juncture the disorder was intense and the Washingtonian's ride to New York was, like Phil. Sheridan's ride from Winchester, to retrieve a lost battle.

The Washingtonian arrived in New York on Saturday morning. He at once went to Mr. Belmont's.   Mr. Belmont was out of town— at Newport, it was stated.   He then went to Mr. Tilden's office, 12 Wall Street, then to his house in East Twentieth Street.   Mr. Tilden had gone out of town—not known whither—supposed northward. He then went to Mr. Augustus Schell's in West Twentieth or Twenty-first Street and saw Mrs. Schell.   Mr. Schell had gone out of town—did not know where—perhaps north—perhaps to Utica.

The Washingtonian then sought Mr. John T. Hoffman, who was the mayor of New York.   Mr. Hoffman was in his office.   He said he knew nothing about the *World* article or its origin, deemed it very unfortunate for the party, and could hardly believe that the Committee had authorized its publication.

The Washingtonian then telegraphed the result of his enquiries and researches to Washington and went to see Mr. Benjamin Wood and other Democratic leaders in New York, from none of whom, however, could he learn the origin of the *World* article. Then, assuming that Tilden and Schell were with Mr. Seymour at Utica, he telegraphed to them there, requesting an interview on the morrow (Sunday) at Mr. Tilden's residence. Finally, as a last resource, he concluded to call upon Mr. Marble and ask him, point blank, what had induced him to adopt the course he had taken. He called at the *World* office on Saturday, October 17th, at about 4 o'clock in the afternoon, and saw Mr. Marble, when the following interview took place:

Washingtonian—"At the request of President Johnson and Marshal Hoover I have visited you for the purpose of asking you some questions with reference to the leading article in Thursday's *World*. Of course you are aware of the unfortunate disorder it has created. We deem it of the utmost importance to know in the first place whether that article was authorized or suggested by the Democratic National Committee, or any of its representative committees, or any member thereof."

Mr. Marble (flushed and nervous)—"I do not admit the right of the President or the Chairman of the Congressional Committee, or yourself, or anybody else, to put any questions to me regarding the course of the *World*. Respect for them and you, however, induces me to say this much: that the Committee had nothing whatever to do with the publication of the article."

This was in some measure avoiding the question. The Washingtonian, without noticing this fact, proceeded:

Washingtonian—"Then let me ask you what was your motive in publishing so extraordinary, uncalled-for, and disastrous an article?"

Marble (getting excited)—"Sir! This newspaper is *my property* and is not amenable to any man or set of men for the course it may choose to pursue."

Washingtonian—"Your declaration surprises me. It was generally understood that Mr. Belmont and others of the party owned a controlling interest in the paper and that it was the organ of the Democratic party. It was certainly trusted as such, and it certainly invited such trust. In view of these facts, I think I have a *right* to ask you for an explanation of the course of the paper."

Marble (thoroughly excited)—"I tell you this paper is my property; *my* property, do you understand? *It has been my property since the first of this month*, and I have neither partners nor shareholders. The *World* is not the organ of the Democratic party nor of any other party. It is an independent sheet, and is entirely at liberty to pursue any course, or print any article it pleases."

Washingtonian (persistently)—"Such may be the position of the *World* now; but it certainly was not its position a short time ago. No intimation was given of the change; and the public was permitted to regard it as still the organ of the party. Such being the case, I again ask you why you printed that article?"

Marble (lashed into fury and losing control of himself)—"Do you want to know why I printed it? Well, you shall know. I printed it to please myself. *I printed it as a sensation article, to give eclat to the paper* and increase its circulation all over the country. Already, the sale of the paper has doubled."

Washingtonian—"That will do, Mr. Marble. No further explanation is needed. What you have already said satisfies my inquiry." And with this the Washingtonian walked away.

To abandon and betray a great political party, that is to say the political principles upon which may rest the fate of a State, for the profits of a newspaper sensation! The motive confessed was worse than any which had been imputed or suspected.

On the following day (Sunday) the Washingtonian repaired to Mr. Tilden's residence and there found assembled Messrs. Tilden, Schell, Church, Hoffman, Seymour, Jr. (a nephew of Horatio) and Col. North, a gentleman to whom had been committed the distribution of campaign documents issued by the Committees.

The Washingtonian explained his mission. It was to obtain from the Democratic National Committee, or their representatives, an explicit and unequivocal declaration with reference to the *World* article. Members of the party throughout the country were at this moment uncertain whether the committee and leaders of the party had authorized or connived at the article, or whether they had determined to abandon the ticket or not. If the Committee were not responsible for the article they should say so unequivocally, and at once.

Mr. Tilden remarked that the Hoover dispatch signed by himself and Messrs. Belmont and Schell was supposed to be explicit enough.

The Washingtonian replied that it was not; tha leaders of the party at Washington still believed that the *World* would not have ventured to publish such an article without consulting with the Committee; that the dispatch had been sent too late, and that the Committee should end all doubt upon the matter by explicitly repudiating the *World* article.

Mr. Tilden intimated that he did not like to make an enemy of the *World*.

Whereupon Mr. Hoffman got up and said very emphatically that that was not the point. The point was that the party throughout the country neeed to be unequivocally assured about the origin of that article so that it might be guided in the course it was to pursue. The gentleman from Washington was quite correct in his views and fully justified in his demands. Messrs. Tilden and Schell, who were the representatives of the Committee, should draw up and sign such a paper as the gentleman had suggested.

After some further objection on the part of Mr. Tilden, who gave way to the Washingtonian's suggestion with evident reluctance, it was agreed that the latter should draw up a dispatch addressed to Mr. W. F. Storey, representative of the Democratic National Committee in Illinois, setting forth unequivocally that the *World* article was without authority or knowledge of the National Committee, or any of its members or representatives; that a change of front was out of the question; and that victory was still assured if the party held together.

The Washingtonian sat down to draw the paper. As he did so, Col. North whispered to him, "I'll venture to say that you will never carry that paper out of this room." To which the Washingtonian replied with confidence: "Oh, yes, I shall get it, and when I do get it, I shall at once put it on the wires."

The Washingtonian completed the paper and handed it to Mr. Tilden, who made some trifling alterations in its diction and passed it to Mr. Schell. It met with the latter's concurrence. Mr. Tilden then signed it; then Mr. Schell signed it. Then the Washingtonian took it up and with a look of triumph at Col. North started toward the door saying: "Gentlemen, I'll just put this on the wires and return." His hand was on the door knob and he was in the act of turning it when Mr. Tilden, running hastily around the table, (this was in the front reception room at the house in East Twentieth Street), seized him by the arm and declared the dispatch ought not to go out without Mr. Belmont's name being attached to it. Mr. Belmont, he explained, was Chairman of the Committee, and it would be slighting him to send the dispatch forth without his signature. He knew

that Mr. Belmont would sign it.   Mr. Belmont was in Newport.   He
(Mr. Tilden) would agree to procure his signature to the dispatch
and send it to Mr. Storey.   It really must be left in his hands until
he could see Mr. Belmont.

What could the Washingtonian do?   Mr. Tilden was not a stranger
to him.   He knew him well and confided in him.   He laid the paper
upon the table and shortly afterward the meeting broke up, with the
express understanding that Mr. Belmont's signature should be procured to the dispatch by Mr. Tilden and that it should be immediately
afterward made public by transmitting it to Mr. Storey in the form
of an official message.

That paper never was signed by Mr. Belmont; never was published;
and to this day the Conservative party has nothing to show that the
World article of October 15, 1868, was unauthorized by the Committee.   The leaders of the party and the masses throughout the
country felt that they had been betrayed, but by whom, whether
Belmont, Tilden or Marble, they could not feel sure.   In this state
of uncertainty and confusion the party went to the polls, leaderless
and demoralized.   Even in this condition it polled 2,648,830 votes
for Seymour against 2,985,031 polled by the Radicals for Grant; and
it only failed of a majority vote by 337,000 or less than 6 per cent.
of the whole number of votes cast.   This 6 per cent. was the reward
of Marble's treachery.

Such is the story of the Crime of 1868, so far as the writer knows
it of his own knowledge.   The connection between its various members is too obvious to need further comment, and the advantages
which the European Syndicate derived from it are to be measured by
the following entirely gratuitous act of legislation:

" In order to remove any doubt as to the purpose of the government to discharge all just obligations to the public creditors, and
to settle conflicting questions and interpretations of the laws by
virtue of which such obligations have been contracted, it is hereby
provided and declared that the faith of the United States is solemnly
pledged to the payment in coin, or its equivalent, of all the obligations of the United States not bearing interest, known as United
States notes, and of all the interest-bearing obligations of the United
States, except in cases where the law authorizing the issue of any
such obligation has expressly provided that the same may be paid in
lawful money or other currency than gold or silver.   But none of
said interest-bearing obligations not already due shall be redeemed
or paid before maturity, unless at such time United States notes

shall be convertible into coin at the option of the holder, or unless at such time bonds of the United States bearing a lower rate of interest than the bonds to be redeemed can be sold at par in coin. And the United States also solemnly pledges its faith to make provision at the earliest practicable period for the redemption of the United States notes in coin." *Act of March 18, 1869.*

This was the so-called Credit Strengthening Act of March 18, 1869. It was passed immediately upon the assembling of the new Congress elected in the Fall of 1868, and was the first act passed by that body and signed by the new President, Grant. By virtue of this act the government of the United States, without any consideration whatever, improved and enhanced the value of the bonds it had issued under the Act of February 25, 1862, and its sequels, which bonds it had sold at half price because of their sale and redeemability in greenbacks. It also, and likewise without any consideration, improved and enhanced the value of the greenbacks, by promising to redeem the same in coin, whereas when they were issued they were sold at half price for war supplies largely on account of their irredeemability in coin.

The passage of this act was equivalent to the payment to various European banking houses, holders of the Five-Twenty bonds, of at least two hundred and seventy-five million dollars, over and above what they would otherwise have received in the form of interest and principal for the bonds which they held or controlled. It really amounted to more than twice as much.

The issues settled by this treacherously procured legislation can never be raised again. The Five-Twenty bonds, whose terms of payment it altered and enhanced in value, without any consideration paid to the government, are now all, or nearly all, paid off. But the men who promoted this measure and who in order to do so cajoled and betrayed a great party which had generously confided its interests to their charge, are not beyond the reach of public censure and reproach.

Mr. Marble In his issue of the *World* dated August 24, 1874, said of himself: "As the editor of a journal which he established, has long owned, and always conducted to maintain Democratic doctrines in government and which, without the assistance of National or State Democratic Committees, has nevertheless come to be everywhere esteemed as in some sense a leading organ of the Democratic party, he has not believed it to be consistent with that implied trust " etc. He here refers with pride to his ownership of the *World* as of long standing. The readers of this treatise will know how long that standing had been; for according to Mr. Marble's own confession it only began about the 1st of October, 1868. He also refers to its independence of Democratic Committees. The only Democratic Committee which had any "support" to contribute until within re-cent years was the Tammany Committee of New York, an organization which cared little for the Democratic party, so long as it could retain its hold upon the profits of the municipal government of that city. From this organization, as appears from the bills and receipts for advertisments, on file with the Comptroller of New York, the *World* received an ample remuneration. As to the National Democratic Committee it had no largess to bestow upon the *World*, which had betrayed and sold it and the party to foreigners. This is the sort of independence of which it boasted.

But the most important of Mr. Marble's statements above quoted is that one wherein he says that the *World* had come to be every-where esteemed as in some sense "a leading organ of the Democratic party," and admits that there was an "implied trust " in the avowal and acceptance of such a position. It will be remembered that in the interview of October 17, 1868, Mr. Marble denied that the *World* was a Democratic organ, in any sense of the word, and that it was under no sort of trust or obligation to support the doctrines or candidates of the party. Afterwards, when he hoped his treachery would not transpire, or had been forgotten, he held that the *World* was a Democratic organ and as such was under an "implied trust " with reference to the doctrines and candidates of the party. And not only in his issue of August 24, 1874, but in many subsequent issues, he sought, and unfortunately obtained, the support and con-fidence of the party, as he had sought and obtained it previous to his treacherous act of October 15, 1868.

———oOo———

THE CRIME OF 1870.

AS TOLD IN THE MEMPHIS MONETARY CONVENTION JUNE 13, 1895.

THE Chairman, Senator Turpie, of Indiana, announced that Hon. Alexander Del Mar, of California, the distinguished writer on Money, was present and would address the Convention. Mr. Del Mar, who was greeted with much applause, spoke as follows:

Mr. Chairman:—Amidst the conflict of monetary theories, doctrines and assumptions which divide the American people—nay the entire civilized world to-day—I can discern but a single principle upon which all parties unite. That principle is stability. Those who hold that like other measures the measure of value should be of dimensions prescribed by law; those who would leave such dimensions to the chances of mining discovery, the vicissitudes of war, or the caprices of fashion; those who are willing to trust the government with the regulation of money; those who have no faith in the virtue or prudence of congress and demand a metallic pledge behind each fraction of the monetary measure; those who regard the whole number of dollars as the measure of value; those who regard the material of each separate dollar as the true measure of value; those who regard money as a legal institution, as well as those who view it only as so much metal—all these alike agree in the cardinal principle that a monetary system, if it is to be just and equitable in its operation, should be stable. It should afford a reasonable assurance to the buyer, the seller, the debtor, the creditor, the producer, the consumer, the annuitant, the pensioner and the wage-earner, that it will work no essential, no violent, no revolutionary, rise or fall of prices, so that men may buy and sell, contract, undertake and plan for the future upon a more or less assured and enduring basis.

This principle, so manifestly just, has obtained not only the assent of extreme partisans on all sides of the present heated controversy, but it is laid down by the most eminent jurists who have devoted their attention to this great institution of social life, it is laid down by Vattel, Grotius, Puffendorf, Montesquieu, Bodin, Dumoulin, Grimaudet; indeed, by all the great modern writers on the principles of law.

It it because I am profoundly convinced that no institution can enjoy a permanent footing in this country unless it is founded upon principles of equity, it is because I believe that any system of money which does not point to substantial stability of prices is destined to speedy overthrow, that I stand here to-day to support so far as my feeble abilities permit the demand for the restoration of the ancient coinage laws of the Republic.

At no time in the history of the world have such enormous, such inequitable, such widespread, I may almost say cosmic disturbances of prices, such unforeseeable and undeserved changes of opportunity and fortune occurred as have occurred since the evil day—now some thirty years ago—when the coinage of silver began to be checked throughout the civilized world.

The fact—which nobody has questioned—that more than half of the combined circulation of all the States of the Occident consists of legal tender paper notes; the fact, which all admit, that over 95 per cent of all the exchanges of the world are transacted not with money, whether of metal or paper, but with mere orders for money, such as checks and bills of exchange—these facts, together with others, prove that metallic coins, though made of both silver and of gold, are quite inadequate to justly measure the parity of exchanges, so that the coins have to be eked out not only with papermoney, but also—and still more largely—with orders and promises of money, which being limited in circulation to one or two persons and slow of movement at that, have to be continually drawn, destroyed and redrawn. In short, the growth of commerce during this century of steam and electricity has been so enormous that the equity of exchanges has come to rest chiefly upon paper money and private orders for paper money, the latter affecting to be exchangeable or promising to be exchanged on demand for coins of gold or silver. Defective and dangerous as such systems have proved, no satisfactory substitute for them has yet been accepted; and like many other institutes inherited from the past, we have been content to patch them up and make them last as long as possible.

What now shall be thought of the man or the men who thirty years ago deliberately destroyed one-half of the scant support upon which the stupendous superstructure of the world's commerce, contracts, and expectations depends? And what now shall be done to further patch that tottering system which—like Dr. Oliver Wendell Holmes's one-horse chaise—threatens to fall to pieces altogether?

Concerning this last suggestion you need no guidance from the mere Historian of money; your minds are already made up; your verdict is determined—the law must be restored. Concerning the history of the demonetization, I am here to unfold it to you, because in it is contained the refutation of those false, venomous and traitorous cries of "interested motives," "dishonest money" and the like, with which the friends of restoration have been assailed.

The Monetary Commission of 1876, with which I was connected, reported that the Acts of 1873 were, one of them, passed surreptitiously, and the other upon false or erroneous assurances. This has since been vehemently denied. I am going to show you not only that the Commission was right, but that these acts were the issue of European intrigue and precedent.

At the period of this legislation the ratio of value at which silver and gold were purchased and coined at the French mints was 15 1-2 weights for 1; at the mints of the United States 16 to 1; In consequence of this difference (about 3 per cent) those who had silver to coin sent it to Paris, rather than Philadelphia, San Francisco or New Orleans. Had the opposition to the coinage of dollars in the two metals and the preference by creditors of the government for one metal over the other been of American origin, the one metal chosen would inevitably have been silver, because in fact the silver dollar was worth 3 per cent more than the gold one, and because the fundholders who notoriously promoted and supported the legislation of 1873 would no more have preferred gold dollars then, than they would silver dollars now. But in France, indeed, in Europe generally, whose mints and markets commonly followed the vast coinages of France, the gold and silver coins of like denominations were of precisely equal value. Hence to the European holder of American bonds in 1863-4 it made no difference whether he was paid in gold or silver coins, provided—and this was the point essentially important to his interest and avidity—provided that the debtor was deprived of the option of paying in coins of the other metal. The preference of gold was certainly not American, because at the American mint ratio gold dollars, when melted down, were only worth 97 cents. It was therefore of European origin. We shall presently see why these "cheaper" dollars were preferred to silver ones.

Under the Code Napoleon it was explicitly laid down that all debts, taxes and contracts for sums of money, no matter in what other terms expressed, were legally and equitably dischargeable in the current money of like denominations upon the day of payment. This principle came down from the Roman Commonwealth; it was preserved by Paulus in the Digest; it was upheld by all the jurisconsults of the Empire and of the various provinces and kingdoms into which the Empire afterwards split; it was supported with great emphasis and erudition by the Privy Council, in the celebrated case of the Mixed Moneys, and it was maintained by the United States Supreme Court in the great cases which were adjudicated by Chief Justices Chase and a full bench.

At the time when the necessities of our government compelled it to issue hundreds—nay, almost thousands of millions of 6 per cent and 5 per cent bonds, with interest payable in "coins," the French Court of Cassation promulgated a decision in perfect accordance not only with the entire range of legal authority, but also with the Code Napoleon, to the effect that on this subject no man could contract himself out of the law; in short, that contracts for money were equitably dischargeable in the current money of the day of payment. This decision alarmed the European holders of American bonds. "What might not those shrewd, those progressive Americans do with respect to the interest on these bonds, which was payable in "coins?" Perhaps they would strike coins of debased gold, like the ancient Athenians, or of pewter and gun-metal, like the princes of the house of Stuart, or plated brass, like the petty lords of modern Germany. Would they not be justified by law, by history, by authority, by precedent, by the decision so recently rendered in the French court of Cassation ? Most assuredly."

There was but one way to avert this financial calamity. This was to demonetise one of the precious metals, and fix the standard of the other. But which metal should be demonetized ? Gold ? "Oh, no, the American government would never consent to that, because it would oblige them to pay in silver dollars, which, under the operation of their own laws, as influenced by our (the French mint) law, are worth 3 per cent more than gold ones. Therefore, let us endeavor to demonetize silver. To us it makes no difference; to the Americans it is a gain of three per cent. Let us bribe them with this three per cent to surrender their option of the metals. All doubt as to kind of payment being then removed, our American bonds, purchased at forty or fifty cents on the dollar, will rise to par and over. A la mort, l'argent !"

At that time there were 1,000 to 1,500 millions of American government bonds in Europe, or held on European account. The inception of this project, which soon developed into an active intrigue, therefore stood to win 600 to 1,000 million dollars.

Such were the circumstances that gave rise to the resolutions adopted by the Latin Monetary Union of 1865. The original proposition emanated in Belgium: it was grafted upon that movement for the unitization of weights and measures, the dissemination of the metrical and decimal systems and other "fads" which were urged throughout Europe by numerous societies with respectable and influential followings. The members of these societies (not the leaders) were like the fat sheep which one sometimes sees marked for slaughter. Their single function in life is to look plump and wait for the butcher. The butcher is usually the practical politician; in this case it was the practical financier.

The Monetary Union of 1865 was the beginning of that scheme of reckless avidity and dark intrigue which in the course of a few years destroyed one half of the metallic basis of money, plunged the commercial world into bankruptcy and pledged it to conditions commercially impossible to fulfill and politically dangerous to endure. These conditions menace the peace of the world. I do not plead for retribution, but for justice. Let the fundholder be paid in gold. He is not the same one who duped and betrayed us in 1868 and 1873, but his assignee, an innocent third party, upon whose title there is no stain of fraud. Let him be paid in gold. So far as the present fundholders are concerned the mischief is done, and it cannot be equitably repaired. But as for posterity whose affairs we are pinning down to the capricious and inadequate limits of a single metal: as for the future stability of contracts, which twenty-five years of catastrophic experience should convince us cannot be secured by means of gold money, I say let us at once restore the ancient law. "The way to resume is to resume!"

From 1865 to 1870 the fundholding syndicate into whose hands it is quite evident this intrigue had now fallen, was incessant in its operations. Numerous conventions under its patronage were held in France, Belgium and Germany: its influence is plainly discernible in the treacherous defection of certain party leaders during the American presidential election of 1868[1]; in the gratuitous "Credit-

---

[1] The Democratic party on the eve of the Presidential election of 1868, when almost certain victory awaited it, was betrayed by Martin Marble, editor of the New York World.

strengthening " act of 1869; in the appropriation clause of Boutwell's
needless Fifteen Hundred Million funding bill; and especially in that
surreptitious and scandalous alteration of the British Mint Code of
1870, which furnished the immediate example, precedent and justification for the analogous alteration of our own Mint Code, namely, the
alteration which demonetized silver and threw the commercial world
into bankruptcy.   It is to the circumstances connected with this
alteration of the British Mint Code that I now ask your especial
attention.

The Mint law of 1816, section 9, the law which closed the British
mints to the private and unlimited coinage of silver, whilst it opened
them to the private and unlimited coinage of gold, left it in the
power of the Crown at any time (by and with the advice of the
Privy Council), to substantially reverse such policy.   In other
words, down to the year 1870 the Sovereign of Great Britain had
the power by proclamation to reopen the mints to the private and
unlimited coinage of silver.

This provision of law appeared in an amended form in section 9
on page 3, lines 14 to 20, of the Mint bill of 1870, next to be mentioned; but it is nowhere to be found in the amended bill, nor in the
statute into which it was erected Following is the provision of 1816,
as amended in the *original* Mint bill of 1870:

Section 9, lines 14 to 20: "Where, after the date in that behalf
fixed by a proclamation under this act, any person or body brings to
the mint any silver bullion, such bullion shall be assayed and coined
and delivered out to such person at the rate of 62 shillings for every
5,760 grains imperial weight, or 373.24195 grammes metric weight,
of silver bullion of standard fineness so brought, in whatever denomination the same is coined."

On February 10, 1870, the bill containing this provision was
brought into the Commons by the Chancellor of the Exchequer
(Robert Lowe) and Mr. Stansfeld.   Its professed object was "to
consolidate and amend the law relating to the coinage and Her
Majesty's mint."   In moving for leave to introduce it, Mr. Lowe
said its objects were merely to "consolidate the rules and regula-
lions of the mint" and abolish the useless office of mint-master, and
thus save £3,500 a year to the nation.   Upon these assurances the
bill was read for the first time and put upon its passage.   The bill
not only contained the provisions above cited; it prescribed the
manner and form in which this privilege of silver coinage might be
exercised.   Section 12 provided that "it shall be lawful for Her

Majesty, with the advice of the Privy Council, from time to time by
proclamation, to do all or any of the following matters, namely"
* * * (clause 7) "to regulate any matters relative to the coinage
and the mint which are not provided for by this act."

These were the only provisions in the bill relating to that royal
prerogative of silver coinage which had been reserved in the Act 56,
George III., c. 68. It is evident that in order to effectually destroy
this prerogative, both section 9, lines 14 to 20, and section 12,
clause 7, of the bill of February 10, 1870, had to be altered. The
former provision was a restriction or limitation of the latter; therefore its repeal (by itself) instead of destroying, would have enlarged,
the royal prerogative. This consideration made it necessary, if the
prerogative was to be destroyed, to deal with both clauses; and this
is precisely what was done. The second reading took place February 25, 1870, when after a brief discussion, during which no inten-
tion was disclosed of destroying or curtailing the royal prerogative
of silver coinage, the bill was committed. When the bill emerged
from committee (March 10), that portion of clause 9, namely, lines
14-20, which might have opened the mints to the coinage of silver, had
disappeared altogether; and no mention of this elimination appears
in the debates reported by Hansard, who simply says (Vol. 199, col.
1730): "Clauses (or sections) 8 to 10, inclusive, added."

In section 12, clause 7, the following italicized words were in-
serted, making the clause read as follows: "To regulate any matters
relative to the coinage and mint *within the present prerogative of the
crown* which are not provided for by this act." The italicized words
worked an entire change of the law. On March 11 this bill was "considered as amended" (no discussion),and on March 14 it passed its
third reading, without discussion.

There was another and very important alteration made, one which
destroyed the power of the Crown to make foreign coins legal tender (this included the Indian rupee) but for the present I propose
merely to deal with the alteration which destroyed the royal prerogative as to the silver coinage of Great Britain.

When it was up for second reading February 25, Mr. Lowe said
that, with the exception of the economy mentioned, the bill proposed no alteration of the law, and, seemingly as an apology for its
length, added that "Her Majesty has very large prerogatives in
the matter of money and if they were not recited in the bill it
might be supposed that we were anxious to impose limitations upon them. * * * The Queen has now, I apprehend, by prerogative,

a power to introduce into any of her dominions any coin she pleases, * * * although such power could only be exercised by proclamation by the Privy Council." When it was up in committee, March 10, Mr. Lowe again said that the object of the bill was not to alter, but merely to "perfect" the law; yet, without discussion and without hesitation, he accepted amendments which not only altered the law, but altered it fundamentally and opened the door to all those consequences which I allude to elsewhere.

In the House of Lords, on second reading, March 18, the Marquis of Landsdowne explained that the bill made "no innovation of any kind, no new principle was introduced in the bill," etc. Upon these assurances it was read and committed. When motion was made, March 22, to go into committee on this bill, Lord Kinnaird remarked that it had "not received due consideration; for it passed through its various stages in the other House after midnight, and *amendments were introduced by members who represented establishments interested in the question.*[1] The noble Marquis of Landsdowne had stated, on the second reading, that it contained no innovation and no new principle." The Marquis of Landsdowne thereupon rejoined that he had said it contained no *important* innovation, with the exception of the clause transferring the mastership of the mint. "But," replied Lord Kinnaird, "I contend that it contains *very important* alterations."

Yet, from beginning to end, neither in the House of Commons, the House of Lords, nor in the committees of either house, was any intimation made of any purpose to curtail the Queen's prerogative of silver coinage, nor did any discussion take place on the subject. Lord Kinnaird was the only person in either house who made more than trivial objections, and as to his objections, they were insufficient to stay the progress of the measure, which partly on this day and partly on March 24 went through the lifeless ceremony of its passage through the Lords. When Lord Kinnaird uttered his last protest, he said he believed that "dust was still thrown by certain parties into the eyes of the deputy master of the mint—not gold dust, for this went into their pockets." But as it is evident that he had not the faintest suspicion of what was really going on, it yet remains to be seen into whose eyes the dust had gathered. On the following day, March 25, the bill was read in the Lords a third

---

[1] This is an obvious allusion to the Bank of England, which, it will be remembered is a private institution with a national name.

time and passed without discussion. On April 4 it received the Royal assent and thus became law.

Within a fortnight after its enactment in England, this Mint bill, which, it was alleged, contained "no innovations and no new principles," was in the hands of the Comptroller of the (paper) Currency at Washington, Mr. John Jay Knox, a young man and a new man, entirely ignorant of coinage, and one whose office had no connection with coinage or the mints.[*] There it became the basis of a bill which purported, like its prototype, to be merely a codification of the existing laws relating to the coinage, but which, also like its prototype, really curtailed and destroyed the ancient prerogative of the State with regard to the coinage of silver and the making of silver coins (national or foreign) legal tenders for the payment of debts. Within the space of a few years similar legislation against silver money was introduced by the same agencies and enacted in the principal states of the Occident; and to-day all the nations of the West and all the people of Europe and America, both born and unborn, are committed not only to the payment of past obligations, but also to the conduct of future transactions, upon the basis of a stock of gold coins which at the present time does not exceed £800,000,000 sterling and which is chiefly deposited in banking establishments, liable to be controlled and, as many people suspect, actually subject to the control of a private syndicate of British and Continental financiers.

Gentlemen of the Convention! You have now heard the story of this sordid conspiracy. It began long before the American silver mines became productive. Its active phase arose out of the issue of five-twenty bonds and the decision of the French Court of Cassation. It gave rise to the Latin Monetary Union. It precipitated the demonetization of silver in Germany and other states. It surreptitiously altered the British Mint Code and in a similar manner and by similar means it secretly and scandalously altered the American Mint Code. It munificently rewarded all those who promoted its objects. It mercilessly attacked all who opposed them. It robbed this country of hundreds of millions. It influenced its politics and it still influences them. It has grown rich enough to lend fifteen millions to the English banks, eighty millions to Italy, ten millions to Chili, and two hundred millions each to Austria and the United States. It controls our foreign exchanges. It has already

---

[*]The original bill had been in his hands from the outset of the intrigue in England.

plunged the commercial world into a long train of disasters and stands ready to repeat the achievement whenever it will pay to do so. Do you want any more of this? (Cries of No! No!) Then let us put an end to it. Let us restore the law, and, if anything further is needed to regulate our monetary system, so that it shall serve, instead of control our commercial prosperity, let that, also, be done, not by entangling alliances with other nations, not under the guidance of hired and traitorous newspapers, owned by foreign syndicates, but according to American ideas, under the Constitution, and subject only to the principles of justice, and the immortal canons of the Civil and Common law. (Loud and long continued applause.)

———oOo———

THE CRIME OF 1873.

WHFN the civil war ended, the federal debt was about $2,800,000,000; the debts of the various states, townships and municipalities, about $1,400,000,000; of railways and canals about $2,500,000,000; and of other corporations about $300,000,000; together about $7,000,000,000.

Between a fourth and a third of this sum was owing to investors in Europe, who had lent or advanced it, in *paper dollars*, which cost them on the average about half a dollar each in gold or silver coins. An equal proportion had been advanced by American capitalists on similar terms. The balance was advanced before the war, or else before the paper currency depreciated; and was therefore lent in coins or their equivalent. Leaving this portion of the debt out of view, it is probably near the mark to say that at the close of the civil war there were owing nearly $5,000,000,000, which cost the lenders (Europeans and Americans), about half that sum in coins.

The whole of this debt was payable, under the act of February 25, 1862, in greenbacks; the interest on a portion of it was payable in coins of gold or silver.

The first move of the lenders after the war closed was to open a newspaper war upon the paper money which they had themselves lent to the government. The greenbacks, it was contended, were "dishonest" dollars; indeed, not really dollars at all, only worthless, disreputable rags, a disgrace to civilization, disseminators of fraud and disease, etc. This question was fought in the Presidential campaign of 1868, in which, by referring to the newspapers of the day, it will be seen that the writer hereof bore no inactive part. As the election day approached every sign indicated the triumph of Governor Seymour, the champion of greenbacks, and the defeat of General Grant, the champion of coins. All of a sudden, on the eve of election, and without a note of warning, the then trusted organ of the Democratic party, to wit, the *New York World*, edited by Manton Marble, but owned, as it was commonly believed, by August Belmont, hauled down its flag, deserted the ticket on the eve of election, and left nearly two million voters to the effects of treachery, panic and disorder.

The first fruit of this nefarious transaction was the passage of a so-called "Credit Strengthening Act," dated March 18, 1869, by which the United States government pledged itself to pay the principal as well as the interest, of its paper debt, in gold or silver *coins.* In other words, without any consideration whatever, it undertook to pay for every paper dollar which it had borrowed, a gold or silver dollar, of the long-established weight and fineness; and by this act and its subsequent action, it compelled all indebted persons and corporations to do the like.

Having by these means secured to themselves the payment of a *whole* metal dollar for each *half* of a metal dollar advanced to the government, thus clearing cent-per-cent profit at a single bound, the conspirators next attempted to double the value or purchasing power of such metal dollars, by means of destroying one-half of them, to wit, the silver ones.

The following is a brief account of their operations: At that time and for several years previously, a government commission had been occupied in the work of revising and codifying the statues of the United States.   The Revision Commissioners being lawyers, and not financiers, merchants, nor metallurgists, were not familiar with the technical branches of administration; therefore they made it a practice to visit the executive departments and consult with the principal officers concerning the practical interpretation and administration of the laws.   When they reached the Mint Bureau, its principal officer had already in his hands a proposed codification of the coinage laws, the model for which had been forwarded to him by certain friends or agents of the Bank of England in London.

This new American Mint Code apparently embodied all the existing laws on the subject, nay, it even purported to follow their very language, and to blend them all into an harmonious whole; but such appearance was deceptive.   This deception is not charged upon the Director of the Mint (since dead), but upon the men who prepared and placed the codification in his hands, some of whom are still living and who will doubtless take pleasure in reading this communication.

The old law (not the proposed codification) made it the duty of the Director of the Mint to receive deposits of either gold or silver; to coin such metal into dollars—the silver ones to contain exactly sixteen times as much metal as the gold ones—and to return the same to the depositor; and it declared all such dollars to be money of the United States and legal tenders for all purposes and to any amount. The public debt was made payable under the act of March 18, 1869, in such dollars, whether of silver or gold. The proposed codification (not the law) dropped the silver dollar. It did not demonetize it, but by omitting to include it in the various coins which the Mint Director was authorized to strike, it was rendered unlawful and impracticable for him to strike any more of them.

As to the means by which this modification was palmed upon the Director of the Mint and afterwards—that is to say, before the Revision Commissioners dealt with it—how it was palmed upon Congress, the subject has been frequently dealt with already. The dupes who afterwards attempted to defend it, utterly failed and are dead; the men who worked the trick are some of them still living and may yet be named and impeached.

The act (embodying the codification) when passed, was not read in both Houses at length, and it is notorious that this transcendant change in the monetary system of the country, affecting the most vital and widespread interests, was carried through without the knowledge or observation of the people.

It was neither demanded by the resolutions of public meetings or political conventions, nor asked for in petitions from electors. As paper money was the actual currency of the country at that time, a coinage act was not likely to attract general attention. While it was pending, the press of the country was entirely unobservant or silent. After it passed, no notice was taken of it for more than two years afterwards. If it had been known that any such vital question as the demonetization of silver was lurking in the bill it would have aroused the most widespread discussion throughout the country; as is shown by the present contest upon remonetizing it; which is only the same question reversed, and which is likely to dominate all other public questions until it is settled. The most striking evidence, perhaps, of the public inattention to the effect of the coinage act of 1873, is the fact that President Grant, who signed it, had no knowledge of what it really accomplished in relation to the demonetization of silver, and was still uninformed about it so late as October 3, 1873, as is proved by his letter of that date to Mr. Cowdrey. In this letter he wonders why silver is not brought to the mints and coined into money! If the President of the United States, in daily intercourse with the public men of the country, had failed to hear during certainly seven or eight months that the laws no longer permitted money to be coined from silver, it must be inferred that ignorance on the subject was general and profound.

It has since been contended by the apologists for demonetization that the word "dollar" was omitted from the enumeration of silver coins in the codification, because the silver dollar had lost value. On the contrary, the French mint was at that time paying about three per cent. more for silver bullion than the American mints; and for this reason, and as a matter of fact, the American silver dollar was at a premium of three per cent in American gold dollars. It has also been pleaded that but comparatively few American silver dollars had ever been coined and circulated; but this plea omits from view the vast number of Spanish silver dollars and of American halves and quarters which were coined and made full legal tender under the American law for two-thirds of a century and which in fact amply filled the metallic circulation of this country.

It has also been pleaded that the American silver dollar was dropped because Germany had demonetized silver. But this is not true. It was dropped by the adoption of the New Mint Code of February 12, 1873, whereas Germany did not demonetize silver until July 9, 1873. It has also been pleaded that the silver dollar was dropped because of the vast quantities of silver produced from the Comstock lode; whereas, in fact, of the entire product of the lode one-half in value was of gold.

All these and other pleas, subterfuges and excuses were invented after the deed was done. The silver dollar was dropped purely and simply to enhance the value of the gold dollar, and thus to double the debt of the American people. That was the motive and there was no other motive. The proof of it is that the very same men (I do not merely mean the same class of men, I mean the identical individuals) who betrayed their party in 1868 and who doubled the public indebtedness by promoting the act of March 18, 1869, assisted to again double the debt, by promoting the surreptitious mint codification act of February 12, 1873, and the further surreptitious act of June, 1874. I quote from the official report of the United States Monetary Commission of 1876, page 90:

"The demonetization of silver coined and uncoined was affirmatively completed in June, 1874, by the following section (3,586) of the Revised Statutes: 'The silver coins of the United States shall be a legal tender at their nominal value for any amount not exceeding five dollars in any one payment.' No law was ever passed by Congress of which this language can be considered a 'revision.' The

Revised Statutes were enacted in bulk.   They were intended to be a revision merely of the existing laws, without change or introduction of new matter, and Congress was *assured* by its Committee on Revision that *no new matter* had been introduced into them.   It was not possible for the members of the committee to have personally verified the exact accuracy of the revision.   They must necessarily have relied upon assurances given to them by the persons actually engaged in the work. [These were the codification or Revision Commissioners previously mentioned.]   Whoever may be responsible for this *error* in the Revised Statutes, the ancient money of the country, instead of being *legislated* out of existence by Congress, was *revised* out of existence."

It will be seen that the legislation of 1865-'74 was no "academic experiment," but a sordid crime, hatched abroad and brought into this country by the treacherous people who governed the utterances of the New York *World*.   Every one of the conspirators engaged in the commission of this crime suddenly acquired riches.   Some of them have since delivered to admiring audiences long dissertations on academic finance, and one of them has been distinguished by an unsuspecting President of the United States with high marks of public preferment.

————oOo————

EQUITABLE MONEY.

Reply of Hon. Alexander Del Mar to Prof. Thorold Rogers' address delivered in the London Chamber of Commerce, March 20th, 1890. (From the *Financial and Mining Record*, April 19th, 1890.)

A SPECIAL meeting of the Chamber of Commerce was held in the Council-Room, East Cheap, on March 20th, 1890, at 4.30 P. M. Sir John Lubbock, M. P., presided. Among those present were Mr. David Howard, chairman of the Council, Sir Vincent Kennet-Barrington, Sir John Coode, deputy chairman, Mr. Herman Schmidt, author of "Tates Cambist," and numerous other distinguished gentlemen.

Prof. J. E. Thorold Rogers, author of "Agriculture and Prices during the Middle Ages," "A Manual of Political Economy," etc., read a paper on "Facts illustrating the epoch during which a double standard was legal tender in Great Britain, 1759—81." The cards of admission to the Chamber contained the following notice: "It is not proposed to enter into the metallic controversy but to deal with the facts as established by past experience. It is, therefore, desired that those taking part in the discussion will confine themselves to facts more than theories."

Prof. Rogers, who was received with applause, occupied about an hour, and said in effect:

He had chosen the period in question because previous to it, from 1714, the government had practically adopted a single gold standard, by overvaluing gold in the coinage: and that at about the end of it, strictly speaking in 1774, Parliament passed an act limiting the legal tender of silver coins to £25. The double standard was in fact a Parliamentary experiment which was tried during three-quarters of the 18th century, doubted during its continuance, and finally abandoned as unworkable. The period 1759-81 comprised 23 years of this period. He had collected from the newspapers of the period the prices of gold and silver bullion, under the respective heads of foreign gold, standard gold bars, Spanish silver coin and standard silver bars. Altogether he presented nearly 2,000 different quotations, He had not averaged them for each year, because he thought that statistical averages were misleading and that each one of these quotations ought to be studied by itself. It would be instructive to work them out. He found an excuse for the fullness of his evidence in the wish that in case the Chamber discussed the figures, they should have all the facts before them and added:

"Now what did these exhaustive facts prove? They proved how seldom the market price of bullion coincided with the English mint prices and therefore what an utter failure the double standard has been. The double standard was merely a plausible hypothesis, an economical generality; and the proposals of the Bi-Metallic league of the present time are an entirely new departure in the theory of currency. The adoption of their views would make a serious addition to all business risks. I do not doubt the good faith of those who believe that government regulation of the two metals has induced uniformity of value; I only question the extent of their information.

"Out of my protracted researches into prices I have had constant occasion to repudiate conclusions drawn by eminent men for whose abilities and integrity I have the sincerest respect, who would have arrived at very different conclusions, if they had possessed the evidence which I have had the good fortune to collect and that at no little pains and expense. I have put a specimen of such evidence before you.

"The ratio of value between silver and gold embodied in the mint price of these metals during the period under review was 15.07 to 1. In the bullion market the ratio at certain dates in 1763 was 14.37 to 14.66; in 1764-5 it was 14.98; in 1772 it was 14.12 to 14.42; in 1778-9 it was 15.07 and in 1781 it was 13.54. Generally speaking silver was at a premium over the mint price. These figures and calculations are essential to the interpretation of the situation. Debtors will inevitably pay in the cheapest metal. The attempt on the part of England to establish a legal proportion between gold and silver was a total failure.

"The existing monetary system of England is a gradual development; it has no parallel in the civilized world; and it smoothly and successfully carries on a system of trade, vast beyond computation. It sprang from sagacity and is based upon a well-grounded confidence. One might well hesitate before tampering with such a fabric." (Applause.)

Mr. DEL MAR rising to reply, spoke rapidly and without notes as follows: "That the Chamber could scarcely fail to be impressed with the enormous industry of Prof. Rogers in collecting the quotations of gold and silver bullion which he had presented to them (applause). However, he could not help expressing regret that the Professor's exertions had been so protracted and his pains and expense so great; for he might have saved them all. The statistics which he claims to have rescued from the columns of ancient and obscure newspapers will be found printed in all of the following modern works: 1st, "An Inquiry on National Currency," by Robert Mushet, of his Majesty's Mint, London, 1811; 2nd, "Executive Document, No. 117, First Session, Twenty-first Congress of the United States of America;" and 3rd, "A History of the Precious Metals" by Alex. Del Mar, London, 1880. These works were all to be found in the British Museum Library, where the Professor had toiled so long upon the *London Courant* and *Lloyds Evening Post.*

What is more, they all gave those annual average prices of bullion which the Professor has affected to despise, but without the aid of which the speaker need hardly remark, life was too short to test the merits of the contention to which they had been invited. (Laughter.)

"Now, what did these quotations convey, not the quotations merely, of twenty-three years selected by Professor Rogers, but the whole period from 1710 to the latest date mentioned by him. Let me run them over rapidly for you.

Table showing the average Decennial ratio of value in London between gold and silver bullion 1710 to 1760 and the average Annual ratio, 1760 to 1774.*

Period.	Ratio.	Period.	Ratio.	Period.	Ratio.	Period.	Ratio.
1701-10	15 27	1761	13 94	1768	14 58	1775	14 62
1711-20	15 15	1762	14 63	1769	14 45	1776	14 34
1720-30	15 09	1763	14 71	1770	14 35	1777	14 04
1731-40	15 07	1764	14 91	1771	14 36	1778	14 34
1741-50	14 93	1765	14 69	1772	14 19	1779	14 89
1751-60	14 56	1766	14 41	1773	14 73	1780	14 43
1760	14 29	1767	14 45	1774	15 05	1781	13 33

*Calculated chiefly from sales of Spanish and other foreign coins and from the foreign exchanges. The decennial averages by Mr. R. H. G. Palgrave in Rep. Royal Com. on Depression of Trade, 1886; the annual averages from "Del Mar's History of the Precious Metals," p. 252.

"From the remarkable regularity of these quotations, it is evident that there was some cause behind which governed them. That cause I will presently endeavor to point out. Meanwhile, let us consider the conditions under which this discussion has been invited.

"In the first place, no notice has been given of what was intended to be argued, beyond what is conveyed by the card of admission. In the second place, this card asks us not to discuss the lecturer's theory, but rather to confine ourselves to the facts which he proposes to adduce. This looks too much like peppering your guest with a concealed weapon after you have got him to tie his own hands.

"What has the Professor himself brought into this discussion? Has he confined himself to facts and avoided controversial theories? Not at all. On the contrary, he has gone back 150 years to select certain market prices, which he appears to suppose had never been collected before and would, therefore, not be questioned now. Upon this ocean of ancient figures he has floated a dozen questionable currency theories. The very title of his paper launches several of them. It is a theory, not a fact, that a double standard was ever legal tender in Great Britain; it is a theory, not a fact, that it was legal tender, during the particular years 1759-81; and it is a theory, not a fact, that the statistics of Professor Rogers illustrate this epoch fairly, or illustrate it at all. Indeed, the very term 'standard' in the sense in which he has employed it, involves a theory. Properly speaking, standard relates to the degree of fineness of coins, as the Sterling or Easterling standard, meaning eleven-twelfths fine. Prof. Rogers erroneously uses it to mean the kind of metal or metals of which coins are made; and by averring that a double standard was legal tender he advances the theory that gold and silver bullion was legal tender in the 18th century; which is not a fact; coins were and are legal tender; money was and is legal tender; but not bullion. You might own a stack of bullion as high as St. Pauls and yet be unable to pay a debt of a single pound ster-ling with it. It would be quite competent for your creditor to re-fuse it and demand money. None of Prof. Rogers' figures are facts, but merely inferences of prices and ratios founded upon quo-tations of foreign exchanges and sales of foreign coins.

  " This confusion of thought and the misuse of nummulary terms here alluded to, is distinctly of modern and recent growth. Thou-sands of books have been written on the subject of money, but in none of them, previous to the 17th century, so far as I am aware, was money ever confused with metals, or metals with money. Metals are the product of God; money is the invention of man. There is no difficulty whatever to distinguish them. Early in the 17th century the King of Spain, after deducting for the Royal Treasury a quinto, or *fifth*, from the production of the precious metals in America, saw fit to open the Government mints to the coinage of all bullion into money without charge to the depositors. In effect, this was a standing offer on the part of the Government to purchase an unlimited quantity of tax-paid gold or silver bullion and to pay for it in coin. It was also an offer to buy coins and pay for them in bullion, weight for weight, in fine metal. A legal ratio of value, namely 13⅓ weights of silver for one of gold, was fixed upon between the metals. As anybody could melt his coins into metal and the Government was always ready to work the metal into coins, it followed that legally, money was now metals and metals were money. This piece of legislation being idiotically regarded by courtiers as the source of Spain s military grandeur and commercial prosperity, it was quickly imitated in Holland about the middle of the century and in England in the year 1666, by the act of 18th Chas. II. ; an act that so far as gold is concerned, is still in force in the British Empire.

"Out of this act at once sprang a new philosophy mis-called political economy; the whole of which, when you come to look at it closely, is based upon the act of 1666. It had no existence before that act and it will vanish whenever that act is repealed. The corner stone of this philosophy is the theory that 'the value of every object or service in demand depends upon the cost of producing or supplying it.'[1] These are the very words of Professor Rogers. So imagining this theory to be incontrovertible and that it applied to gold as well as to commercial products, he seeks to-day to show you how much superior the theory is to the act of Parliament which offered to buy 15 silver for 1 gold or 1 gold for 15 silver! This is strange logic. Here is a theory, in fact the mere spawn of one Act of Parliament, but which the economists, conceitedly imagining it to be their own precious offspring, have held to be superior to all acts of Parliament. The tenacity with which they hold to this remarkable conclusion, presents a rare case of paternal pride. (Great laughter.)

"Yet the gentleman who throws around us this theory and so many other theories, says he wants facts, not theories. He is a seller of theories and a buyer of facts. But need I remind him, in the words of Buckle, that a mere accumulation of facts, without knowing or explaining the relations between them, is the work of the pedant; not that of a philosopher? The paper which he has read to us defines his position on this point even better than the card of admission. It is not that he is averse to theories, but to other people's theories; for he has given us plenty of his own. (Laughter.)

"It is a theory that England adopted a 'gold standard' from 1714 to 1759, and a 'double standard' from 1759 to 1774; it is a fact that both gold and silver coins had been full legal tender in England substantially since the 13th Century and this continued down to 1816.

"It is a theory that Parliament in 1774 limited the legal tender of silver coins to £25. It is a fact that this provision only applied to worn and clipped coins. Good silver coins remained full legal tender as before.

"It is a theory that the concurrent use of gold and silver money was an experiment, either ephemeral or otherwise, or that it was abandoned as unworkable. It is a fact that full legal tender gold and silver coins have circulated side by side in nearly all countries since the dawn of history and that in fact at the present moment

[1] Professor Rogers; "Manual of Political Economy," Chap. III.

there is more silver coin employed as full legal tender money in America, than there is gold coin in England.

"It is a new and startling theory that statistical averages are misleading. On the other hand it is a well known fact that *selected* statistics are worthless.

"It is a theory that the figures of Prof. Rogers present all the facts of the case he has brought forward. How few facts they do present will be shown hereafter.

"It is a theory that the discrepancy between some of those figures and the English-mint prices of bullion proved the concurrent use of gold and silver coins to have been a failure. It is a fact that the quotations obeyed the prices of that and other Government mints which competed at the time for the purchase of bullion.

"It is a theory that the concurrent use of gold and silver coins was a hypothesis, or an economical generality, or that the proposals of the Bi-Metallic League constitute a new departure in currency. It is a fact that this system of money is of the highest antiquity and that it has been found difficult to devise a better one. What this country wants, what every progressive country wants, is a system of money which shall conform to the requirements of equity. What is wanted is an Equitable Monetary Measure, a measure of value fixed in volume, either absolutely or relative to population, or to some certain other mark of growth. We neither want the limitless greenback of the ignorant, nor the dwindling gold currency system of the pedantic. What the expanding trade of this great empire demands is a sound and uniform money for all its domains; and nothing better than the concurrent use of gold and silver coins with paper adjuncts, all of full legal tender, has yet been devised for it. The dislocation between the British and Indian currencies at the present time is a serious menace to British commercial prosperity.

"It is a theory that the use of silver money would add to business risks. On the contrary, it is a fact that these risks, owing to the fluctuations of exchange, were never greater than at present and were much less so previously to 1873, down to which year the French and American mints were open to the purchase of all of our silver, at a fixed price in gold. (Applause.)

"It is very kind of the Professor not to doubt the good faith of those who decline to accept his theories. He evidently regards their refusal as a mild form of lunacy, which is only to be cured by studying his own original and 'protracted researches' into the prices of bullion, with some thirty printed pages of which he has

just favored us. Now that he is made aware that others have pre-
ceded him in these researches and that concerning them they came
to entirely different conclusions, perhaps he will give his adversaries
credit for practical sense as well as good faith, and forthwith join
the ranks of Currency Reform.

"It was a theory (both of Aristophanes and Gresham) that debtors
pay in the cheapest metal; it is also a theory that they pay in any
metal at all. The law obliges them to pay in money; and unless the
mint insanely choosed to turn their metal into money for nothing,
the metal would not avail for payments at all. These petty theories
are not laws of Nature, but the by-products of old acts of legislation,
which will disappear the moment the pruning knife of reform is applied to the subject.

"It is a theory that the monetary system of England has no parallel
for merit or that it is the product of sagacity, or that it smoothly and
successfully conducts our trade. The facts are that its groundwork
is the treacherous mint act of 1666 and the idiotic one of 1816; that
it has never worked successfully; that at the present moment it depresses and threatens the entire British trade with the East; that it
has broken up many Lancashire industries; that it is cutting the
ground under the feet of British agriculturists and working men;
that it is driving the bullion trade to America and has seriously im-
paired the power of the Bank of England to draw in emergencies
upon the bullion supplies of the world; and that if not very soon
repealed by our going back to the old system of gold and silver payments, we will have to suspend coin payments altogether and adopt
greenbacks for money.

"The gentleman advances another theory, viz.: that the cost of
producing gold and silver governs their value. Did he ever calculate this cost; did anybody else ever calculate it; is it at all calculable?
To all of these questions my reply is a decided No; and I challenge
a contradiction. The gentleman says in his 'Manual of Political
Economy'—and these are the theories he has brought with him here
to-day—that 'gold and silver are produced in nearly equal quantities by nearly equal labor, or at nearly equal cost; and that in the
rough it may be said that the cost of producing a pound of gold is
fifteen times as great as that of producing a pound of silver, and
that therefore a pound of gold is worth about 15 pounds of silver!' What
is the gentleman's opinion of the intelligence of this Chamber that
he should imagine it could swallow such cheap diet as this? The
fact is that the vast metalliferous product of Spanish America, of

Japan, of India, of Brazil, was obtained by Europe chiefly through plunder and slavery. After the Spaniards and Portuguese had plundered it from the natives, the English and the Dutch plundered it from the Spaniards and Portuguese. This is what distinguished Drake, Morgan, Raleigh, and the other maritime adventurers of the 17th century. They captured the Spanish plate ships at sea, or sacked the mining camps and bullion depositories on the Spanish Main, and the product came into the markets for sale. You might as well calculate the cost to the burglar of producing your silver spoons when he breaks into your house and steals them, as try to calculate the cost of this bullion to Europe. (Loud laughter and applause.)

"Though a member of this commercial Chamber, I have followed the business of gold mining for many years and am practically familiar with the conditions surrounding the production of the precious metals. Moreover, I have conversed with hundreds of intelligent mining men, who had gone into the subject very carefully, but I never yet met one who could tell me what was the average cost of producing gold or silver, nor can I imagine what it is, even approximately. Will the gentleman pretend to say that he can calculate it either from the statistics of former times, or the return of the mining companies which have been recently floated in London? (Great laughter, in which Prof. Rogers joined.) We have had 600 mines brought to us from California, Nevada and Colorado, and 1,200 from Australia, and goodness knows how many more from Mysore and South Africa, each costing us several hundred thousand pounds. Does the gentleman derive his idea of the cost of producing the precious metals from the experience of these companies? (Applause.)

"I hope it wasn't like that of a friend of mine, who one day showed me a gold button, weighing perhaps a quarter of an ounce, which he said had cost him £200,000. The Comstock was probably the richest lode ever discovered, and consisted both of gold and silver. It yielded the enormous sum of £60,000,000; yet it cost no less than £300,000,000. Both the product of California and Australia cost in labor alone several times as much as it fetched at the mints. During the days of plunder and slavery the precious metals cost little or nothing; at the present time they cost much more than their value. The immense stock left from the old times depresses the value of the new supplies.

"If it be asked why such an unprofitable industry is continued, why gold and silver mining is carried beyond the limit of prudence, the answer is: Because mines cannot be found at pleasure and because

no man owning a mine knows when to stop, for the next stroke of
the pick may bring him a fortune. He is buoyed up by hope; hope
in a gambling industry, in a lottery, in a mere football of fortune;
for such is gold and silver mining. When anybody says that he has
calculated and knows the cost of the precious metals on hand in the
world, I simply turn my back upon him; for I know that he has not
done so, and he does not know what they cost. The calculation is an
impossible one, because every ounce added to the stock on hand
changes the value both of the old product and of the new. And
this fact is not only a proof that such a calculation is impracticable;
it also proves that the value of these metals depends upon their
quantity and not upon their cost of production.

"If the cost of production theory was sound, there could never be
a general rise of prices; indeed, many of the economists, finding
themselves logically forced into this stupid conclusion, have actually
made it an article of their faith, and asserted as a fact, what was
merely a logical deduction and one that their own observation belied.
Adam Smith is among this number. In one place he denies the
possibility of a rise; yet in another place he most emphatically notes
that general rise of prices which actually followed the Plunder of
America. Said he: 'The discovery of the abundant mines of
America seems to have been the sole cause of this diminution in the
value of silver [money] in proportion to that of corn. It is accounted
for in the same manner by everybody; and there never has been any
dispute either about the fact or about the cause of it.'"

Prof. Rogers (interrupting)—"Please repeat that."

Mr. Del Mar, after repeating Adam Smith's words,[9] continued as
follows:

"Having thus shown the fallacy of some of Prof. Rogers' theories,
I now turn to some of his bullion quotations and the lessons they
teach. I said that their extraordinary regularly indicated a govern-
ing cause behind. I will now state what that cause was; and as this
appears to have entirely escaped the observation of the learned Professor, perhaps the next time he comes up to London to teach the
subject of money to the Chamber of Commerce, he will come better
prepared. (Laughter.)

"At the time to which he alludes, namely, 1759 to 1781, there were

---

[9] In his "Manual of Political Economy," Chap. III, Prof. Rogers said that during
one half of the 16th Century, the value of silver (money) fell more than one-half,
which is only another way of saying that there occurred a general rise of prices—precisely what Adam Smith said.

five or more governmental mints open to the purchase of silver in gold coins and of gold in silver coins. The prices paid for bullion by these mints, or the ' ratio ' between the metals, was altered by legal enactments from time to time, and was rarely or never the same in any two of these countries simultaneously. There was sharp competition for bullion; a cutting of rates. The ratio in Spain in 1740-50 was 14.244 silver for 1 gold; in 1775 this was changed to 15½; in 1779 to 15.8. The ratio in Portugal was fixed by the act of 1688 at 16; in 1747 this was changed to 13⅓. The ratio in France was fixed by the act of 1726 at 14.46 and this lasted until 1785, when it was changed to 15½. In Holland the ratio was from 14¼ to 14½. In England the ratio was fixed in 1717 at 15.2 and this lasted until 1816. The Professor says it was 15.07, but this difference between us is of no practical importance. Here are nine different prices offered for bullion and for bullion in any quantity. Confining ourselves strictly to the 23 years selected by the Professor, we have six different prices offered by the principal producing and coining nations of the period. The extremes of these prices are 13⅓ on the one hand and 16 on the other. In face of all this competition the Professor wonders why silver did not stand petrified at 15.07, which was mere the English mint price! He says he wants facts not theories. Well, here are facts. The fact is that five different nations were bidding for bullion at the same time; the fact is that they bid six or more different prices; the fact is that the lowest price for gold, viz., 13⅓ was bid by Portugal from the year 1747 onward; and the highest price, viz., 15.8 was bid by Spain from the year 1779 onward; and the fact is that the so-called market price in London fluctuated between, but never moved beyond, these limits. It was like a pendulum vibrating in a clock case; yet the Professor not only wonders why it did not stand still, but also why it didn't go through the case! These aberrations in the price of bullion may be marvels in the world of political economy, but I can assure the gentleman that they are quite explicable in that of every-day fact and of common sense." (Loud applause.)

Mr. Del Mar was followed by Mr. Hermann Schmidt and others.

INDEX.

CHARLES II. ASKING PARDON OF BARBARA.
Pepys' Diary, 1667. From a picture by W. P. Frith, R. A.

www.ingramcontent.com/pod-product-compliance
Lightning Source LLC
Chambersburg PA
CBHW030545270326
41927CB00008B/1512